International Wing Chun Organization
www.hkwingchun.com
www.iwco.info
www.wingchunelements.org

Willow in the Wind
Wing Chun's Soft Approach

by Grand Master Donald Mak

2016

First Published March 01, 2016
Copyright © 2016 by Donald Mak, www.hkwingchun.com

ISBN-13:978-1523994960
ISBN-10:1523994967

layout & design Valeriu Secareanu, Claudiu Cucu

Willow in the Wind
Wing Chun's Soft Approach

Contents

Updated Foreword

Originally, this book was to be published in the early 2000s, but owing to the commitments of a full-time job, I had little time to find a publisher, and so the project was literally put on the shelf for the past 15 years or so. Because of the lengthy interval between the times I wrote the book and today, I gave up any intention of publishing it since it was written more than a decade ago – and a lot of things have changed since. For example, the premises of my Sifu's school (Grandmaster Chow Tze Chuen) at Hung Yue Mansion was sold, my own school's name was changed from the Hong Kong Wing Chun Institute to the International Wing Chun Organization, and I retired from my full-time job. The saddest event was when one of my students, Mr. Williams Lee, who partnered with me in preparing the photos for compiling teaching notes, passed away.

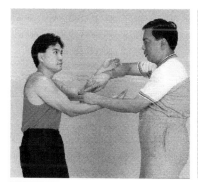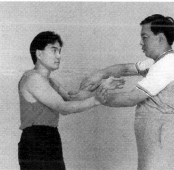

Williams Lee partnered with me demonstrating the changing hand position during Pun Sao

Not only have events taken their course, but also my own thinking and views on Wing Chun have evolved as well such as the fighting approach of using side body, throwing and grappling techniques. Given all this, there was no point in making any efforts to publish this book, or so I thought. Thanks to my grand-student, Claudiu Cucu, who introduced me to the latest publishing technology and to the encouragement of many of my Wing Chun friends and students who have found the contents of this book valuable, I have decided to share its contents with the wider Wing Chun world, although, at the end of the day, the views and concepts described in the following pages merely reflect my own Wing Chun insights of some 15 years ago. I am currently writing other Wing Chun books and hope that this will only be the start of an entire series of books I plan to write on Wing Chun in the years ahead.

Donald Mak, Sifu
12 March 2015
Hong Kong

Foreword by Chow Tze Chuen, Sifu
Yip Man Wing Chun, Hong Kong SAR

Original Handwritten Foreword

代序

"人事有代謝，往來成古今。" 先賢此說，莫不道盡世間萬千事物的規律。詠春界亦非例外。捱滾了半世風雨，驀然回首，先師已逝，而新輩朋出，不禁慨然感嘆，可憐白髮生。

而世上之為賢者，不管是聲名赫赫抑或寂寂無名，都不甘泯泯然淡出江湖，而提在有生之際，代謝之前，窮一己之力以為後人留得更多財富。憶昔葉問宗師在香港教授詠春拳，第一次讓世人有機會認識和接觸到這門一直秘而不宣的優秀武學，就是一個很好的範例。至于他精心致力，言傳身教，培養出一批又一批後秀，將詠春拳開枝散葉，傳播發揚到世界各地，以成就今日之根基和局面，更是對詠春界一個很大的貢獻。因此得益之人，何止百萬！而在芸芸受益人當中，我亦算其一了！

我追隨葉問宗師研習詠春拳是從一九五三年開始。當時其武館設在油麻地利達街。在一九五七年大概在我學至尋橋套路時，武館移至李鄭屋村，其時武館的設施極差，地方狹窄，既多風扇，甚至連洗手間都沒有。由于條件不理想，師兄收徒很少，我便將我九龍巴士公司的工友都介紹過去。在這段期間，我每課必至，風雨不改，從師兄身上習得詠春的整個系統課程，包括拳套，木人樁，步法，腳法，八斬刀和六點半棍。因地方淺窄，館裏安裝不了木人樁，我就在九龍徑的小屋的陽台上

安了一個。從此師父就親侍我木人樁的八

節膀路。我於獲益至鉅。每天下班後勤練不輟。

由于木樁密集安裝、附間長了身上及其周圍

都長了瘀苔。一經下雨便消不了而練習時

非留神定氣不可。久之覺不經覺間練

就了馬步和步法的穩健。

在香港我是第一個跟師父學得八斬刀的。

記得師父在教授時用的是一雙木刀。如

期間有人入館叙授必即停止。

一段時間後師父見我勤奮好學基礎

與入品俱佳、遂將我提為助教、常領後

來的師兄弟。到了一九六三年間、師父的武館

搬到了平山道興業大廈、我原本想繼續

追隨師父。但遠的他卻要求我自立門

戶。為鼓勵和增添我的信心、師父為我的

武館特地從慈州買來了一副木樁。這副

木樁的股杆雖然已較更換教次。其主幹

卻一直使用至今。亦是微此時起、我就

遵照師命開始了業餘授藝的生涯。這

今雄址已幾易。

我云授藝。非求謀財聚富、亦非求聞達

於人。只願不負師託、為繼承傳播、和發揚

師父的寶貴技藝盡一份綿力。為達成這

一份使命、我多年來不發鬆懈、輝竭竭力地

提高自身水平和培育後入。在這苦心之下

教出的徒弟多有不少技藝求色的。如周國華

陳德光、劉中興、戴老達、張宗偉、黃振球等、自

皆已授成出師。而其中有名麥廣權者、自

一九七九年以來二十年間風雨不改地追隨本入

左右。勤勉而虛懷蹈實而聰敏、不耻于下問。

不倦于研習，終盡數學得我之心法和詠
春拳之精粹。因可証言一句，能代表我
本入盼授諸書泰之盼有者，僅其一人
而已。

然而廣權並不滿足於此。他文化素質
好，善於將我盼授內容加以歸納與整理
使之更為條理化系統化和科學化，對
本館的教學起到很大的促進作用，在
深刻領悟本門法理的基礎上，通過自身
的實踐亦時有創造，形成自己的特色。
在我的引導下，他在近年來也業餘參
與教學，一方面通過教學相長以求精
益求精，進一步探求詠春奧秘，另一方
面亦為在育人上助我一臂之力。他言傳身
敎，實事求是，在授課時經常給學生作

語橋來提高他們的感性印象，有了他協
力，我研究成先師的遺願就更有信心了。
聞得廣權有著述之意，以將本門之要
結合其多年來實踐之心得必諸同好
我大感歡慰，並不避筆墨粗疏，欣然作
此序，作為廣權的師父，我了解其為入
深知其功底，反清楚其能力之盼及，因而
有理由相信，此書的問世，對詠春界也
好詠春愛好者也好，必然是一件好事
對提本入來說亦就我所不能繁我達
成了一橋心願，希望它能不負使命抛
磚引玉，使更多的入能夠受益或得到
啟發，為詠春拳的發展起到應有
的作用。

是為序

一九九九年八月廿六日

鄧××

代 序

「人事有代謝，往來成古今」，先賢此說，莫不道盡世間萬千事物的規律。詠春界亦非例外。披灑了半生風雨，驀然回首，先師已渺，而新輩朋出，不禁慨然感嘆，可憐白髮生。

而世上為賢者，不管是聲名赫赫抑或寂寂無名，都不甘混混然淡出江湖，而趕在有生之際，代謝之前，窮一己之力以為後人留得更多財富。憶昔葉問宗師在香港教授詠春拳，第一次讓世人有機會認識和接觸到這門一直秘而不宣的優秀武學，就是一個很好的範例。至于他精心致力，言傳身教，培養出一批又一批後秀，將詠春拳開枝散葉，傳播發揚到世界各地，以成就今日之根基和局面，更是對詠春界一個很大的貢獻。因此得益之人，何止百萬！而在芸芸受益人當中，我亦算其一了！

我追隨葉問宗師研習詠春拳，是從一九五五年開始。當時其武館設在油麻地利達街。在一九五七年大概學至「尋橋」套路時，武館移至李鄭屋村，其時武館的設施極差，地方狹小，既無風扇，甚至連洗手間都沒有。由于條件不理想，師父收徒很少，我便將我九龍巴士公司的工友都介紹過去。在這段期間，我每課必至，風雨不改，從師父身上習得詠春的整個系統課程，包括拳套、木人樁、步法、腳法、八斬刀和六點半棍。因地方淺窄，館裏安裝不了木人樁，我就在九華徑的小屋的陽台上安了一個。從此師父就親傳我木人樁的八節套路。我如獲至寶，每天下班後勤練不輟，由于木樁露天安裝，時間長了，身上及其周圍都長了青苔，一經下雨便滑不可耐，練習時非留神定氣不可，久之竟不經覺間練就了馬步和步法的穩健。

在香港我是第一個跟師父學得八斬刀的，記得師父在教授時所用的是一雙木刀，如期間有人入館，教授必即停止。

一段時間後，師父見我勤奮好學，基礎與人品俱佳，遂將我提為助教，帶領後來的師弟，到了一九六二年間，師父的武館搬到了青山道興業大廈，我原本想繼續追隨著師父，但這時他卻要求我自立門戶。為鼓勵和增添我的信心，師父為我的武館特地從廣州買來了一副木樁。這副木樁的肢杆雖然已被更換數次，其主幹卻一直使用至今，亦是從此時起，我就遵照師命開始了業餘授拳的生涯，迄今館址已幾易。

我之授拳，非求謀財聚富，亦非求聞達於人，只願不負師託，為繼承傳播和發揚師父的寶貴技藝盡一份綿力。為達成這一份使命，我多年來不敢鬆懈，殫精竭力地提高自身水平和培育後人。在這苦心之下，教出的徒弟有不少技藝出色的，如周國華、陳德光、劉中興、戴志遠、張宗偉、黃振球等，皆已技成出師。而其中有名麥廣權者，自一九七九年以來，二十年間風雨不改地追隨本人左右，勤勉而虛懷、踏實而聰敏、不恥于下問、不倦于研習，終盡數學得我之心法和詠春拳之精粹。因可証言一句，能代表我本人所授詠春拳之所有者，僅其一人而已。

然而廣權並不滿足於此，他文化素質好，善於將我所授內容加以歸納與整理，使之更為條理化、系統化和科學化，對本館的教學起到很大的促進作用，在深刻領悟本門法理的基礎上，通過自身的實踐亦時有創造，形成自己的特色。在我的引導下，他在近年來也業餘參與教學，一方面通過教學相長以求精益求精、進一步探求詠春奧秘，另一方面亦為在育人上助我一臂之力。他言傳身教，實事求是，在授課時經常給學生作活樁來提高他們的感性印象。有了他協力，我對完成先師的遺願就更有信心了。聞得廣權有著述之意，以將本門之要結合其多年來實踐之心得公諸同好，我大感歡慰，並不避筆墨粗疏，欣然作此序。作為廣權的師父，我了解其為人，深知其功底，更清楚其能力之所在，因而有理由相信此書的問世對詠春界也好、詠春愛好者也好，必然是一件好事，對我本人來說，亦就我所不能，幫我達成了一樁心願。希望它能不負使命拋磚引玉，使更多的人能夠受益或得到啓發，為詠春拳的發展起到應有的作用。

是為序

鄺子傳
一九九九年八月廿六日

Foreword by Chow Tze Chuen, Sifu
Yip Man Wing Chun, Hong Kong SAR
English Translation

For what we have today, we must thank our ancestors; for what was transmitted becomes our heritage today. Our ancestors said "the essence of innumerable matters is impossible to discover and attain within the limits of a lifetime". Wing Chun is no exception to this. The first half of my Wing Chun learning was spent in hardship on the fundamentals. It suddenly comes to mind my teacher Yip Man Sifu saying in the past with a deep sigh that when new generation of friends come out, pity the older generation who are neglected.

In a world that places value on new talent and ignores and isolates the old regardless of reputation, the old soon fades into obscurity. As age catches up with me, I would like to thank my ancestors and wish my very best to my descendants and hope that they in turn would leave behind an even richer legacy.

I recall the past when my master Yip Sifu was teaching in Hong Kong for the first time and exposed this once secretive and first rate martial art, giving the public the opportunity to learn it. Yip Sifu was an exemplary and devoted teacher who gave personal and detailed instructions, cultivating batches after batches of students.

Under Yip Man Sifu, Wing Chun Kuen was spreaded to the far corners of the world. This in itself is a massive achievement and contribution to the art of Wing Chun. The learning of Wing Chun has benefited millions and I count myself as one of the fortunate ones.

I started learning from my sifu Yip Man in 1955. At that time the association was located at Lee Tat Street in Yau Ma Tei. In 1957 when I was learning the Chum Kiu form, our association was relocated to Li Cheng Uk Estate. The new school in Li Cheng Uk was narrow and compact. There was no fan as well as washroom. Due to the poor facilities, the intake of new students declined and I introduced my colleagues from Kowloon Motor Bus company where I worked to come learn from Yip Sifu.

During this period, I attended every lesson regardless of whether it was rain or shine. It was due to Sifu that I was able to master the entire Wing Chun system which includes the forms, dummy, footwork, knives and pole. Due to the limitation of space, we were not able to fix a dummy inside the school. I then setup a dummy at the balcony of a small house situated in Kau Wah King.

It was here that Sifu transmitted the eight section dummy form to me. This to me was like obtaining a precious gemstone. I trained continuously on the dummy during my leisure hours after work. Prolonged exposure of the dummy to the weather resulted in green moss growing on the dummy trunk as was the area surrounding the dummy. On days that it rained the ground became unbearably slippery. During training my mind had to be concentrated and keeping the chi steady. By accident I also found that this helped greatly in the training of the stability of my stances and footwork.

I was the first one to learn the knives from Sifu in Hong Kong. I remembered that Sifu used a pair of wooden knives to teach me and if anyone came into the school lesson had to be stopped immediately.

Due to my diligence and willingness to build my Wing Chun foundation, I was later promoted by Sifu to assistant instructor to help with the teaching of my junior kung fu brothers who joined later. In 1962, Sifu shifted his school to Hing Ip Building in Castle Peak Road.

I had intended to follow Sifu to the new school, however Sifu wanted me to set up my own school. In order to encourage and give me confidence, Sifu specially bought a dummy from Guangzhou. for my school. Although the dummy's limbs have been changed many times, the dummy trunk is still intact and is used till today. It was from that time onward that I began my part-time career as a Wing Chun instructor as requested by my Sifu. The address of the association had changed a few times since then.

In teaching Wing Chun the seeking of wealth and showing off of skills is not my cup of tea. What I care about is not putting down other teachers' merits and achievement. As inheritor of my Sifu's teachings, I try my best to spread and enhance my Sifu's precious skills. To uplift my own skill and to bring up the new generation, I have not slackened my efforts all these years in order to fulfil my Sifu's assignment. After much hardship and suffering I have cultivated a couple of outstanding and skilful disciples such as Peter Chow, Stephen Chan, Hercules Lau, Tai Chi Yuen, Cheung Chung Wai and Wong Chun Kau and others. They have mastered my skills and are currently teaching. Donald Mak is among them.

For twenty years since 1979 Donald has been learning from me diligently, humbly, modestly and dependable. A bright and agile learner, Donald was not ashamed to ask questions nor weary of analyzing and practicing. Over the years he has eventually obtained the essence of my Wing Chun. Thus Donald is able to represent me well in the teaching of Wing Chun and worthy of this testimonial.

However, Donald is not satisfied at just that. With his cultural quality, Donald is an expert at gathering my information and organizing them systematically and scientifically. This improves greatly the teaching in our school. It is through his own practice that he is able to understand the depth of the fundamental methods and theory. It is also through this that Donald is able to create and form his own distinctive characteristics. In recent years Donald has also been involved in part-time teaching under my supervision. It is through the long teaching, he was able to strive for excellence and thus explore the mysterious essence of Wing Chun. On the other hand, he is also a great helping hand to me. Donald teaches personally and with verbal instruction. He acts like a live dummy when doing Chi Sao with his students in order to cultivate their sensitivity. With Donald's assistance, I have confidence in fulfilling my Sifu's wish.

Donald had intended to gather his knowledge and practice through the years and put them into a book to share with everyone. When I came to know of it, I feel consoled and glad. It is also my pleasure to write this foreword with my unrefined words.

Being Donald's teacher, I understand his character and know the depth of his power and clarity of his ability. I have reasons to believe that this book will certainly be good and beneficial for the Wing Chun community and to other practitioners who love Wing Chun as a martial art. To me this is like fulfiling something that I was unable to fulfil. The feeling is like Donald has helped me to fulfil my wish which is unabled to be fulfilled by me. I hope Donald is able to carry on the mission by introducing the art so that more people will benefit from his inspiration and develop Wing Chun to a certain aspect of usefulness.

Chow Tze Chuen, Sifu
Wing Chun Chuen Kwoon
26 August 1999

CINE ASIA

IN THE LAST GREAT WAR ONE MAN DEFIED AN EMPIRE...

"REMINISCENT OF
BRUCE LEE IN
FIST OF FURY"
TWITCH

IP MAN

MENTOR OF ICONIC LEGEND
BRUCE LEE

2-DISC ULTIMATE EDITION

Introduction by Checkley Sin | Producer of Ip Man Movie
Chairman of Wing Chun Union

S hortly after I shot the first Ip Man movie in 2007, my SiFu Ip Chun and Francis Wong suggested me to organize a worldwide Wing Chun Union to coordinate Wing Chun enthusiast in order to further the promotion and development of Wing Chun. In organizing the World Wing Chun Union, Sifu Kwong Kuen Mak, Donald (麥廣權) who is the disciple of master Chow Tze Chuen (鄒子傳) contributed a lot to the Union, therefore made the Union very successful. Sifu Donald Mak is one of the most respectable Wing Chun masters who I know for more than ten years.

In recognition his great contribution and famous standing in the Wing Chun World he was elected to be the Vice Chairman of World Wing Chun Union as well as the executive member of Technical Committee and chief referee of the Union since 2009.

Thenceforth, Sifu Mak has done a lot to the Union. It includes the set up of European Wing Chun Union together with his disciple, Sifu Anatoly Beloshchin. Sifu Anatoly is the President of European Wing Chun Union who has helped his SiFu to promote Wing Chun in Russia and the adjacent countries. The students and grand students of Sifu Mak have actively joined many Wing Chun competitions and won a lot of gold, silver and bronze medals in different Wing Chun competitions. The number of the medals

Sifu Checkley Sin in the center of the first row, photo taken in the celebration dinner together with the Hong Kong athletes after the World Wing Chun Cup 2015 held in St Petersburg

they won is always one of top team in every competition. Right now the schools of Sifu Mak's lineage spread over the Russia and many countries of the Europe, Middle East and Asia with thousands students.

Because of Sifu Mak's masterly Wing Chun kung fu, he was invited to be one of the Wing Chun consultants in Ip Man movie series; Ip Man - Before the Legend, Ip Man - the Final Fight. It helped to make the action of the movies more popular by the audience and attracted much applause of the Wing Chun fellows.

I am very pleased to hear that Sifu Mak is willing to share his masterly Wing Chun secret to the public by writing a Wing Chun book without any reservation. The book has revealed a great deal of information on kicking and footwork, which are the less-touched topics in the Wing Chun circle. It is definitely a valuable contribution to the Wing Chun community that the Wing Chun enthusiasts should read.

Being the chairman of Wing Chun Union, I would like to express my sincere thank to Sifu Mak's selfless contribution to the promotion of Wing Chun and generous share of his Wing Chun knowledge to the general public.

Kwok Lam Sin, Checkley
Producer of Ip Man movie
Chairman of Wing Chun Union
22 May 2015

Introduction by Y. Wu
Nanyang WingChun Singapore
Republic of Singapore

I t is said that the late Grandmaster of the Hong Kong Wing Chun school, Yip Man, was an adept in using the little seen but deadly kicks of the Wing Chun system. In the course of my learning and also researching for "Complete Wing Chun – The Definitive Guide to Wing Chun's History and Traditions" I have had the opportunity to be exposed to different interpretations of the Yip Man school of Wing Chun over the years.

It is said that in Wing Chun the hands and legs should be used together to strike the opponent at once. However my perception is that most practitioners tend to use the hands and legs separately or incidentally so much so that Wing Chun today is more well known for its hands than kicks. It is rare indeed to find a Wing Chun practitioner or school that can utilize the hands and legs freely. After meeting and touching hands with Donald Mak and his teacher, Chow Tze Chuen Sifu, it is my opinion that they are able to convincingly demonstrate this unique aspect of the Yip Man Wing Chun system.

Aside from the kicks, Chow Sifu's lineage is also skilled in what I can only term as the soft approach. Unfortunately the word "soft" has been misused so much that I should explain myself here and the easiest way is to describe what Chow Sifu was like in applying his skills.

In moving Chow Sifu was like the wind - he was here, there and everywhere. In the Chinese box office hit movie about the great Wing Chun master Leung Jan "The Prodigal Son" which Sammo Hung the famous Hong Kong movie star and star of the U.S. television series "Martial Law" starred in and directed, his character of Wing Chun master Wong Wah Bo had jokingly referred to Wing Chun as a style that is based on the movements of an octopus. These words came to mind when I tried out the skill of Chow Sifu at his invitation in free sparring. At the advanced age of 75 (in 1999), Chow could strike freely, accurately and quickly with either hands or feet without missing a beat or running out of breath. In defending Chow Sifu was like a shadow – he seemed to be there but yet not there. He could make me miss by the merest movement of his body so much so it was as if he had never moved.

A main concern of every teacher of the martial arts is that the teachings can be passed on to the next generation. Donald Mak, a long time disciple of Chow Sifu has successfully mastered the teachings of his teacher and empowered to carry on the teachings to the next generation.

It therefore gives me great pleasure to introduce to the reader "Willow in the Wind – Wing Chun's Soft Approach", a ground-breaking book on the soft methods of Wing Chun by Donald Mak Sifu. I am proud to call Donald my good friend and senior in Wing Chun; and would like to thank him for sharing his art with me.

Congratulations on the publication of "Willow in the Wind".

Y.Wu
author "Fundamentals of NanyangWingChun – the official textbook"

co-author "Complete Wing Chun – The Definitive Guide to Wing Chun's History and Traditions"

Introduction by J.M. Manzaneque, Ph.D.
Asociación Española de Wing Chun Clásico
Málaga, Spain

I met my dear friend Donald, the author of this excellent book, through the Internet in 1996. Back then, I had just begun to surf the internet and was trying to collect information regarding some students of Yip Man in whose lineages I was particularly interested to find out more about. The lineage of Chow Tze Chuen, under whom Donald has studied for almost two decades, was one of my main targets at that time.

It was with this in mind that I saw an entry in a Wing Chun guestbook signed by my now very close friend Donald, identifying himself as a practitioner from that lineage. I wrote to him immediately to inquire on the technical characteristics of his line and, very soon, we found ourselves discussing all manner of aspects about Wing Chun on a regular basis and exchanging diverse material related to our styles. This communication and exchange of information has never ceased and lasts now for many years uninterruptedly.

In the beginning, our discussions mainly focused on comparing the technical features of his lineage (Chow Tze Chuen) and my own (Victor Kan). So, we centered on studying and analyzing in detail the differences and similarities of our systems in relation to forms, chi-sao, stances, etc. After some time, however, we also commenced to share information on the other lines coming from Yip Man and, eventually, we included the other lineages out of the Yip Man family into our discussions.

Although in that time I had already heard about some of these other branches, especially Pao Fa Lien and Yuen Kay Shan, it was really Donald, the author of this very interesting book, the person that introduced them to me by sharing what he had seen and researched from his privileged position in Hong Kong. With his great enthusiasm and vast knowledge, not only did he introduce the lesser-known Wing Chun lineages to me but also awoke my curiosity much further. My interest in these rare branches grew to a point that I myself embarked on their research; this interest is still very much alive today.

It is funny that now when I think in retrospective of those early Wing Chun discussions I began with the author a while back, I must indeed admit I could have never envisaged that what started as a simple curiosity would end up entailing an exchange of such a tremendous amount of information and that such a deep friendship would develop from that.

I remember with great pleasure the day when the author and I finally met in Málaga, the "paradise city" of southern Spain. There, for the first time we were able to exchange ideas in a more practical way. Fortunately, time had come for action! At last we were able to see what we really meant in our discussions; and indeed we did, though quite often this meant displaying Wing Chun techniques not just in the Kwoon but also in restaurants, cafes, etc., much to the amusement of the bystanders.

The author´s skills were (and are) impressive, above all his footwork, which is, in fact, an outstanding feature for which his lineage is well known. Donald has the uncommon ability of being able to conjugate a very mobile and incredibly fast footwork with a permanently strong rootedness, elements which, on its own, are already hard to develop but when combined and displayed simultaneously, as the author does, makes it an extraordinary feat to attain. I recall that other Kung-Fu friends from Málaga also joined our exchange training and, from the different perspective of their own styles, all agreed on the very high level of "Kung-Fu" the author has achieved.

The author´s serious and genuine dedication to Wing Chun has produced this book, and it must be good news for the people of his Wing Chun family. I think that Donald´s knowledge coupled with his impeccable gentlemanly manners make him not only an exceptional representative of the Wing Chun art but an honour for his lineage. This book is an excellent contribution to the Wing Chun world and I highly recommend it to all Wing Chun stylists and martial artists.

J.M. Manzaneque, Ph.D.
Asociación Española de Wing Chun Clásico
Málaga, Spain
January 2000

Introduction by Sifu Darrell Jordan
Lee Gar Lin Ving Tsun Athletic Association
Florida, USA

initially began my Martial Arts training in 1967 in New York City with boxing, and in 1968 I began formal training in Shotokan Karate. At the time in New York, there were no Ving Tsun schools to speak of. I had learned about Ving Tsun Kung Fu in 1972 while serving in the Marine Corps in South East Asia. Although I continued my karate training overseas on Okinawa and the Philippines, I was fascinated by this Bruce Lee guy and Ving Tsun who was so popular at the time. Upon returning to NYC, I found the Ving Tsun school of Master Lee Moy Shan, who was one of the first to open a school for the general public in 1974.

Sifu Darrell Jordan is the first one from the left of the top row

Having now been involved in Ving Tsun for the past 25 years, my interest and desire to know more about Ving Tsun is still strong. I have at least picked up and perused every book ever written on the subject, as well as articles in magazines, but quite honestly, I hardly read any of them, nor have I bought that many books on the subject. For the most part, a lot of what is said I already understood, or, it didn't make any sense according to the Ving Tsun theories and principles. So, therefore, I gain nothing by making the purchase. The Ving Tsun theories and principles serve as your guideline, by knowing your Ving Tsun theories you will immediately know how well the author of a book or article understands Ving Tsun. Of course, if the author does not understand them as well as you or better, I prefer not to waste my time and money.

I had traveled to Hong Kong in March of 2001 for the purpose of interviewing the Ving Tsun Grand masters. My idea was simple. The Grandmasters are getting older, and we, especially in America, just do not have the privilege to see them, hear them, nor interact with them in any way. My Sigung Grandmaster Moy Yat passed away in January of that year and this actually served as the catalyst to interviewing the Grandmasters for this reason.

One particular interview was for me of great interest. It was with Grandmaster Chow Tze Chuen. I was introduced to G/M Chow Tze Chuen by my Sihing Master Buick Yip. After arriving to his school, I was introduced to Master Donald Mak, and Master Mak interpreted the interview for G/M Chow and me. No sooner after the interview began, G/M Chow asked me to stand up and he began demonstrations of his Ving Tsun. I would throw a punch and he would move, counter with a hand or foot, or with both simultaneously in the blink of an eye. Again and again I would throw out a technique and I would in turn have fingers pressed into my throat, and eyes, or kicks to my groin or knee. Meanwhile, the counter techniques of G/M Chow were done with little effort and with an ever-present smile on his face.

Master Donald Mak and I became close friends, and continue to this day. Our mutual endeavor is to bring quality Ving Tsun to the world. Master Mak does this by way of this extraordinary book, "Willow in the Wind, Wing Chun's soft approach." He holds nothing back, and truly embellishes on the essence of Ving Tsun leg and footwork like no other book has to date. The leg and footwork of Ving Tsun is greatly ignored by a majority who practice Ving Tsun. It takes dedicated training to gain the advantages of this level of ability. Without reservation, this is the finest book on Ving Tsun ever written. This is without a doubt worth your time, and will be one of those books you prefer not to loan out. Enjoy.

Sifu Darrell Jordan
Lee Gar Lin Ving Tsun Athletic Association
Florida, USA
October 2001

Preface by Donald Mak, Sifu
Hong Kong Wing Chun Institute
Hong Kong SAR

Sifu Chow Tze Chuen and Donald Mak

Our lineage of Yip Man Wing Chun began with Chow Tze Chuen Sifu. Born in 1925, the year of the Ox in Chinese calendar, Chow Sifu first joined Grandmaster Yip Man's Wing Chun school in Lee Tat Street in the Yau Ma Tei district in Hong Kong in 1955.

A few months later another trainee joined the school. This trainee was destined to be the most famous martial artist of the 20th century and named by Time Magazine in the 1999 June 14 edition as one of the top 20 people on its list of "Heroes and Inspirations". WIth a short body of works including the classic movie "Enter the Dragon" before his untimely early demise, the late Bruce Lee also got his start in Wing Chun here.

In 1957 Grandmaster Yip Man shifted his school from Yau Ma Tei to Li Cheng UK Estate. Sited in one of the poorest and oldest public housing in Hong Kong, living conditions in the new school was deplorable, claustrophobic, incessantly hot and basic sanitary amenities was absent. Because of this, few students followed Grandmaster to the new school and new enrollment was low. To help out Grandmaster Yip, Chow Sifu organised a class comprising his colleagues from the Kowloon Motor Bus Company.

During the Li Cheng UK Estate period, Chow Sifu who had reached Chum Kiu level before the move from Yau Ma Tei, attended class daily and was taught the complete Wing Chun system by Grandmaster Yip Man covering all the boxing forms, wooden dummy form, long pole, kicking techniques, footwork and Bart Cham Dao form. This period spanned the years 1957 to 1962. Chow Sifu was also assisting Grandmaster Yip in teaching newcomers.

An interesting story lies behind Chow Sifu's learning of the wooden dummy form. As land in Hong Kong is limited, consequently living area for public housing was very small as it is still today. Because of this constraint, the wooden dummy could not be installed in the school. Rather Chow Sifu overcame this obstacle by installing the wooden dummy in the terrace of a small house at Kau Wah King. Grandmaster Yip then imparted to Chow Sifu the eight sections that comprise the wooden dummy form.

To achieve a flawlessly high standard of performance, Chow Sifu could be found drilling the wooden dummy form every evening after his work shift. Such was Chow Sifu's dedication in mastering the wooden dummy that he even turned a disadvantage into an advantage. The wooden dummy was situated on an area grown with moss. Whenever it rained the damp moss would result in a slippery surface which made it difficult to move about without slipping. Despite this hazard, Chow Sifu took this as an opportunity to develop the precision and strength of his stances and footwork.

Chow Sifu was one of the first few disciples to be inducted by Grandmaster Yip Man into the hitherto highly secretive Bart Jarm Dao form. Grandmaster Yip Man used a pair of wooden knives for teaching. Though the form was taught and its relationship to the boxing forms was mentioned, application of the knives against other weapons was not taught. Grandmaster Yip would also stop instruction whenever someone else came in while teaching was ongoing.

The entire Wing Chun clan from the Kowloon Motor Bus Company taken at the Chinese New Year feast on the 20th of March 1961.

Come 1962, Grandmaster Yip Man moved his school to Hing Ip Building in Castle Peak Road. Chow Sifu was encouraged by Grandmaster Yip Man to strike out on his own as a teacher of Wing Chun instead of following Grandmaster Yip to the new location. To encourage Chow Sifu and give his blessing, Grandmaster Yip presented Chow Sifu with a wooden dummy that he had bought from Guangzhou for Chow Sifu's new school. From this point on Chow Sifu carried on the transmission of Wing Chun on a part time basis until today.

Wooden dummy bought by GM Yip Man still in Chow Sifu's kwoon; dummy trunk still intact though the arms and leg have been worn out and replaced a few times.

Grandmaster Yip continued to refine Chow Sifu's skill even as Chow Sifu was teaching on his own. Grandmaster Yip would visit Chow sifu to see how his class and teaching was getting on. During the course of his many visits, Grandmaster Yip taught Chow Sifu a separate wooden dummy section that focussed on kicking. Grandmaster Yip encouraged Chow Sifu to blend in more sparring and defending techniques in the Chi Sao exercise saying that "Lut Sao Kin Kung Fu" (literally: the real kung fu is seen in free sparring). This means that the Wing Chun practitioner can check his own standard and progress in his training through his ability in free sparring practice. After Chow Sifu finished teaching class for the day, he would go out for Dim Sum with Grandmaster Yip and took the opportunity to learn more from the Grandmaster.

Chow Sifu's started his first class on the roof of a building in Kowloon City. Thereafter he shifted twice; first to Kwai Lin Street in Shamshuipo and later to another building in Butt Street in Mongkok. In 1975, the school was moved to a building in Camp Street in Shamshuipo. The 1980's saw two more shifts – to Ap Liu Street in Shamshuipo and finally to its present location in Hung Yue Mansion in Castle Peak Road.

A soft-spoken person, Chow Sifu had been quietly carrying on the mission of spreading the teaching of Grandmaster Yip Man's Wing Chun without asking for personal gain and fame. Though he has been teaching for the past few decades, Chow Sifu continues to hone his skills by practicing his boxing forms daily. Chow Sifu carries on the tradition by transmitting the complete Yip Man Wing Chun system that was taught to him by Grandmaster Yip.

It is my fortune to have learned from Chow Sifu for the past 20 years. In 1979, I was introduced to Chow Sifu by my senior, Mr Leung Ping Sang who was learning from Chow Sifu then and still is today. The first four years Chow Sifu taught me the three boxing forms of Siu Nim Tao, Chum Kiu and Biu Jee in addition to chi sao and footwork exercises. From 1983- 1985, Chow Sifu taught me the wooden dummy

Tan-Pak Front Slant Kick, One of the kicking techniques extracted from the Kicking section.

form in its entirety together with kicking techniques. Thereafter I spent the next two years learning the Wing Chun long pole and Bart Jarm Dao form. From 1987-1992 I was the assistant instructor for the Wing Chuen Alumni Association. In 1992 I established the Hong Kong Wing Chun Institute to promote and teach Wing Chun on a part time basis until today.

Chow Sifu has been a great inspiration in my learning of Wing Chun and I wish to thank Chow Sifu for giving me the opportunity to learn and receive authentic teachings from him. Chow Sifu is truly a generous and great master.

It is my sincere desire to make known to the public the authentic teachings of Grandmaster Yip Man as transmitted by Chow Sifu during the period spanning the mid 50's to the early 60's. This is my contribution to the Wing Chun world and I do this not for any gain but for love of an art that has given me so much. Teaching Wing Chun is not my career and I am currently employed full time as a director for a commercial organisation in Hong Kong. Practicing and teaching Wing Chun is my hobby and I hope the reader would also share with me this very unique culture of our great Chinese civilization.

The objective of this book is to reveal the theories, principles and methods of our lineage of Wing Chun in resolving conflict by using a soft rather than hard approach. To this end I will outline our general approach to using body structure to neutralize and footwork to dissolving a strong and powerful attack. Please note that this book is not a "how-to-do-it" primer for beginners. Rather it is written for the Wing Chun practitioner who has reached the wooden dummy learning level.

I would like to thank the following people for their contribution to making this book possible:
My Sifu, Chow Tze Chuen – for his selfless teaching and guidance, without which this book would not have been possible. Mr Y. Wu for writing the introduction and drafting the text. Dr Juan M. Manzaneque and Mr Darrell Jordan for their help with the introduction. My students – Mr Thomas Mok, Mr Sarfield Ng, Mr Williams Lee and Mr Michael Chu for their assistance in helping me publish the book. My brother-in-law, Mr Marco Kong – for posing as my partner in the action photos. My wife, Alice – for her support and encouragement in this project.

Donald Mak, Sifu
Author
December, 1999

Chapter 1
The Way of the Willow

1.1 Why Use Soft Approach

It was said that Wing Chun Kuen was created by a nun, Ng Mui and founded by Yim Wing Chun, the daughter of a curd bean shop owner. Although this piece of history cannot be verified, it may have an implicit meaning that Wing Chun is a martial art that is designed for women or physically weaker people who are unable to resort to physical strength alone to overcome a physically stronger attacker.

Notwithstanding whether Wing Chun Kuen is a martial arts system that was founded by a female or not, what is certain is that Wing Chun Kuen is a martial arts system that possesses the characteristics of the internal martial arts. The Chinese internal martial arts are systems of martial arts that rely on non-resistant yielding to overcome a strong attacker. The criteria of internal martial arts system will be described in Chapter 2.

An old poem on the use of softness in the martial arts states:

"Softness is the mind of a willow
which turns the force of the wind against itself"

The idea of softness is likened to that of borrowing strength akin to a willow tree yielding and bending in the face of strong winds during a violent storm rather than resisting the powerful onslaught of the stronger wind. By not resisting, the willow tree can still prevail and live another day whereas trees that refused to yield may not survive intact and may even be broken and/or blown over. The principle of not resisting and yielding is consistent with the principles of internal martial arts.

As the martial arts were developed to enable the weak to defend themselves against the strong, the method of turning the bully's strength against himself is a more feasible and viable method than just resorting to brute strength to resolve the situation. Moreover not every man or woman is built tall, strong and/or heavyset. The soft approach is the weaker person's equalizer against a strong attacker.

1.2 The Wing Chun Soft Approach

The Wing Chun Kuen of Chow Tze Chuen Sifu as was transmitted to him by Grandmaster Yip Man is based on this idea of using softness to overcome hardness.

The willow tree is our chosen metaphor for illustrating an intelligent method and strategy for overcoming a stronger force. To grow into a willow tree, the seeds of a willow tree must be planted. From the seeds of a willow spring strong roots, upright trunk, supple branches and leaves. These are the basis for utilizing the concept of yielding like a willow.

In actual practice and application, the hands can be regarded as the leaves and branches that form the first contact point with the stronger force. By harmonizing with the direction of the force, the opponent's force can be lead to emptiness without violating the structural integrity of the Wing Chun practitioner just like the way a willow tree's branches and leaves would yield to a strong wind yet remain standing. Secondly the Wing Chun practitioner's body can be likened to that of the willow tree's trunk - upright and structurally aligned so as to be able to receive the opponent's force internally and redirect it by using the waist or rechannel into the ground through the legs.

The third basis for yielding like a willow tree is the development of strong roots that allows the Wing Chun practitioner's body to be stable and not easily swayed into an unbalance position by an external force.

Wing Chun's soft approach is mainly actualized by the following maxims:
Loi Lau Hui Sung (Retain What Comes, Escort What Goes);
Ying Siu Bo Fa (Structure Neutralizes, Footwork Dissolves);
Yun Kiu Lok Bok (Lead force into emptiness by aligning it to shoulder).

1.3 Structure Neutralizes, Footwork Dissolves

The approach outlined in this book is consistent with the Wing Chun maxim "Ying Siu Bo Fa, Ying Fu Sung Yung" (Structure Neutralizes, Footwork Dissolves; Attacks can be handled with less effort). This maxim points out the importance of having good body structure and footwork.

The book is designed to explain how this maxim translates into practice and application both for striking with the hands and legs. Section 1.4 explains how to use this book for maximum gain.

1.4 How To Use This Book

The mastery of essential fundamentals coupled with the keys to soft yielding are akin to the bending and swaying of a willow tree during a violent storm is what makes

Wing Chun Kuen an intelligent and superior form of soft martial art.

This book has been arranged such that the essential concepts and principles are explained in the following sequence.

Chapter 2
Seeds of Wing Chun
How does a willow tree come about? Obviously from the seeds of another willow tree. To "grow" into a willow tree, the right seed must be planted.

This chapter covers the essential fundamentals which form the foundations upon which all else resides. The reader should read this chapter carefully as the material covered in Chapters 3 - 5 are conditional upon a firm grasp and understanding of the basics outlined here.

Chapter 3
Neutralizing with Structure
The topic of structural integrity is an important one in Wing Chun. In this chapter the development of a good structure and how it relates to the principle of using softness to overcome hardness is covered.

Three main themes are touched on:
• the branches as a metaphor for hands that give way in the onslaught of a charging bigger and stronger opponent without violating the integrity of the centreline
• the trunk - upright and aligned to receive the opponent's force by redirecting using the waist and legs
• the roots allow the body to be stable and not easily susceptible to the opponent's strength

Chapter 4
Dissolving Using Footwork
In this chapter the use of footwork as derived from the Chum Kiu and Biu Jee form, is discussed. The use of footwork becomes of paramount importance when the opponent's force is stronger than what one's static structure is able to absorb.

Under such circumstances the opponent's force is neutralized by using body turning with the body weight distributed 100% on the rear leg coupled with the shoulder path alignment. Alternatively the Wing Chun practitioner could also step into another more favorable position from which to counterattack while simultaneously making the opponent's attack fall into empty space short of its intended target.

Chapter 5
Shadowless Kicks
The little seen kicks of Wing Chun for which Grandmaster Yip Man and Chow Tze Chuen Sifu are well known for are introduced here.

The concept for being able to kick without telegraphing one's intention to do so, the ability to kick at any time without having to readjust one's balance first, the combined use of the hands with kicking are all explained in this chapter.

The relatively known training methods for developing the deadly shadowless kicks of Wing Chun are introduced here for the first time.

Appendix 1
Examples of Applications
In this section, numerous examples of how the Way of the Willow is used in overcoming a stronger opponent is illustrated.

All examples of applications shown is consistent with the materials outlined in Chapters 2 - 5.

To get the most from this book it is highly recommended that the reader read Chapters 2 - 5 carefully to get the gist of the discussion. Each chapter is linked to the other chapters to present a comprehensive picture of what Grandmaster Yip's method of Wing Chun as taught by Chow Sifu emcompasses.

By following the above format of study, the reader can understand and gain a better working insight into the traditional method of Wing Chun as transmitted to Chow Sifu by Grandmaster Yip Man.

Chapter 2
Seeds of Wing Chun

2.1 Relaxation

Wing Chun is classified as a high level martial art that emphasize the internal aspect of using the body in combat. As an internal-based art Wing Chun especially stresses the importance of relaxation.

What is relaxation? The idea of relaxing the body is much bandied about in any discussion of the internal Chinese martial arts. However, the concept of relaxing is sometimes misinterpreted as letting the body go limp. This is not the case with proper relaxation.

Thus we give our interpretation of relaxation as "not using unnecessary muscular exertion that does not contribute to the efficiency of the movement in achieving its objective".

How does relaxation figure in the practice and application of Wing Chun?

Let's examine the definition of an internal-based martial art and see how Wing Chun fits in. A martial art that is internal in nature is defined by four maxims :

"Yuk Yau But Yuk Keung" (move in a yielding manner rather than in an antagonistic manner) – this means that the Wing Chun practitioner should never go head on against an opponent. The reason is that in being soft the Wing Chun practitioner will be able to absorb and neutralize a much stronger force. This is consistent with the principle of decreasing momentum in physics by increasing the time of collision between two objects so as to decrease the resultant impact force.

"Yuk Shun But Yuk Yik" (move in harmony rather than against the flow of force) – to move directly against the opponent's line of motion is to collide head-on with the opponent's force. This is not an economical use of the body's resources. However, if one could intercept the opponent's line of motion gently, join with the movement and from there lead the

opponent's movement to emptiness, the Wing Chun practitioner will minimize the effort needed to overcome the opponent. By joining rather than pushing the opponent's attacks away, the Wing Chun opponent also psychologically and physically reduces the opponent's natural propensity to resist and induces him to open up to defeat.

"Yuk Ding But Yuk Luen" (move steadily do not move erratically) – to maintain the centreline in the face of an onslaught is crucial in the strategy of Wing Chun as a martial art. By moving steadily and calmly rather than erratically the Wing Chun proponent can control the centre of motion better and force the opponent to take a longer route to unleash his attack. In this way the opponent wastes time and with an edge in timing and positioning the Wing Chun practitioner can prevail.

"Yuk Jui But Yuk San" (move to converge rather than diffuse out) – in Wing Chun the use of the Yee Jee Kim Yeung Ma and Body Squaring allows the practitioner to focus his entire body mass by convergence. The principle of convergence ensures the Wing Chun practitioner's body resources and efforts are not dispersed with the body moving in different directions. This minimizes wastage.

From the above we can see the importance of relaxation as a fundamental principle in Wing Chun as an internal-based martial art that is based on the four principles of Soft (Yau), Yielding (Shun), Steady (Ding), and Convergent (Jui).

In this chapter we have covered the basic building blocks of Wing Chun. As these principles may be difficult to visualize through words and pictures alone, readers will get better understanding on these concepts if it is explained in person.

2.2 Centerline
In Wing Chun, the most important principle is that of the centerline commonly known as "Chung Seen" in Cantonese. The centreline is also referred to as "Jee Ng Seen".

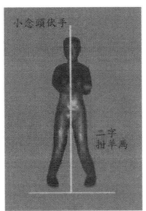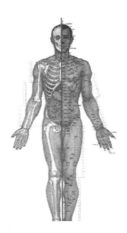

Centerline (or Chung Seen)

"Contact Point align to "Jee Ng"

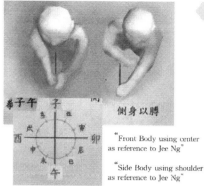

"Front Body using center as reference to Jee Ng"

"Side Body using shoulder as reference to Jee Ng"

The human body can be divided into a left side and a right side. The line dividing the body is rightly the center of the body. So, it is an imaginary line running down from the middle of the body. With this centerline, the body can be further divided into six parts after adding three horizontal lines, one at the top of head; the second one at the stomach area and the third one at the groin area.

These six parts of body (Upper right/left; Middle right/left, Lower right/left) are fundamental to all parrying, deflecting, and blocking in kung fu, particularly in the art of Wing Chun.

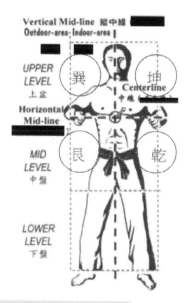

Division of Body

An attacking technique, straight punch starts from and places in front of the centerline

The centerline serves as the base from which all defense and attack are deployed.

One must always have one's centerline guarded with one's hand(s) at all times. Whenever the position of hands changed, regardless of the new position of the hands, one must always endeavor to protect the centerline.

From the perspective of Chinese medicine, in the center of the body from the top of the head right down to the perineum lies a vertical strip known as the Ren meridian. A number of the body's most vital points lie along this strip namely the acupoints baihui, shenting, xuanguan, renzhong, tiantu, shenque etc.

詠春 念頭

Wing C   au

From the western medicine point of view, the body's most vulnerable points are the nose, chin, throat, sternum, solar plexus, gut and groin – all of which also lie on the center of the body.

A defending technique, Bong Sao places in front of the centerline

2.2.1 Importance of the Centerline

The centerline is so important in Wing Chun that it could rightly be called the art of defending and attacking the centerline. The maxim "Man Fat Gwai Chung" (literally: ten thousand techniques originate from the centerline) best describes the importance of centerline.

For the purposes of attacking and defending we need to understand the concept of keeping the vulnerable targets away from the enemy's strikes while bringing our own strikes to bear on the opponent's targets. For this purpose the Wing Chun ancestors have an interesting maxim that goes "bo lay tou, tit kiu, mien fa tu" (glass head, iron bridge, cotton belly).

The implication of this maxim is that the head is an extremely vulnerable and fragile object that should be kept safely away from getting hit as the head is liken to glass which can easily be shattered if struck with the right amount of force and penetration. On the other hand, the arms are hardened like iron rods which can weather the wear and tear of battle while the cotton belly is soft and force-absorbent.

With the above in mind we can understand now why it is so important to defend the center of the body during combat. The rationale for defending the body also applies to attacking the center of the body.

Moreover, with respect to attack, the centerline functions as a mental crosshair for aiming a precise attack at the opponent and also as a constant homing device when chasing the opponent.

| 1) Cross hands down; | 2) Cross hands up |

2.2.2 Defining the Centerline

How is the centerline defined physically?

Simply extend and cross both wrists in front of the solar plexus with the wrists about a fist distance away from the body. Then push both wrists downwards slantingly and stop when the elbows are about 1.5 to 2 fist distance away from the body. Finally with both wrists still touching bring them vertically upward while still keeping the elbows bent and at the same distance as before away from the body.

You have just defined a range for the centerline which is used in Wing Chun for attack and defense.

2.2.3 How to Guard the Centerline?

In Chinese martial arts, the area in front of the body is termed the front gate, just like the literal gate of a house through which one must enter if one wants to get inside (of course it is also possible to enter by the side gate ceteris paribus).

The hands at the area of the wrist define the first gate through which one must enter in order to cross the courtyard. The elbows define the entrance to the house itself. Once the opponent's arms get past the entrance of the house one is extremely vulnerable to strikes as the mind will not be able to process any visual or tactile sensation fast enough to neutralize the attack.

Elbow is placed on the Centerline to defend the punch

Thus, the best position for the arms/hands in guarding the body is by aligning both the elbow and wrist in front of the centerline. However, if one is forced to open the front gate either by the opponent's strike on the arm or a voluntarily change of the hand position, the entrance to the house viz the elbow must be shut in order to prevent the opponent's attack from coming through and landing on one's body.

Thus to be successful in attack and defense one must be very precise in knowing where the center is constantly in order to manipulate the changes that tend to occur in the heat of combat.

2.3 Static Elbow

A common admonishment heard in Grandmaster Yip Man's class was for the student not to keep the elbows too close to the body or too far out. The elbows must be kept static in front of the centerline even if the arms are pressed or the entire body moves. This is the principle of the static elbow, one of the cornerstones of the Wing Chun system.

The principle of the static elbow requires the elbow be kept down and at a reasonable relatively constant distance from the body such that attack and defense is not compromised yet one is still able to effectively counterattack.

A static elbow allows for:
- *Protection of the body without having to retract the arms back every time i.e. the body is constantly protected during the different phases of combat*
- *Positioning of the entire body's mass behind the arms for generating force i.e. during striking*
- *Minimize unnecessary arm movement by keeping the arms in the optimal position from which attack and defence can originate in the fastest, shortest possible manner without telegraphing*

In the absence of the static elbow principle the following are the consequences:
Elbows too near to body – in this position the arms are weak as the structure is collapsed. Consequently the arms are unable to maintain the necessary structural integrity to intercept and neutralize a strong force. Also as the arms are overly bent, one cannot neutralize or change from one position to another without being struck by the opponent's arms which are now too close to one's body for comfort.

Elbows too far from body - the body is exposed unnecessarily if the elbows are over extended; this situation is more acute for close range combat where one would not want to be caught with the body opened to blows unnecessarily. Also since the body mass is out of line with the arm, it is impossible to throw a forceful strike that maximizes power; as most of the power is coming mainly from the arm with underrated contribution from the body which is out of alignment with the striking arm. To realign the body behind the arm would require additional time; which could be hazardous since split second timing can determine the outcome in fast moving combat.

2.4 Body Squaring

In performing the movements of Wing Chun, the principle of keeping the body square while facing the opponent is a must.

What is Body Squaring?

In Wing Chun the principles of the system require that attack and defence should go hand-in-hand instead of being separate movements.

Body Squaring

This principle means that :
1. the same hand that is defending also carries out the attack as an immediate follow-up, 2. one hand handles the defence whilst the other hand attacks.

For the latter the only way both hands can carry out this function effectively is to keep both hands equally out in front of the body. Only then can any of the hands shift easily between the function of attack and defence.

Secondly the principles of Wing Chun involve the use of a simple two-dimensional equilateral triangle for targeting the opponent. The use of a simple geometrical shape for referencing one's own movements for intercepting and counterattacking eliminates guesswork as to how one's hands and legs should move and be placed in relation to the opponent's in order to seek and maintain the advantage.

Thirdly, keeping the body square provides for a measure of stability in motion. During the dynamic phase of combat, a body that is in motion can be unbalanced easier than when it is at rest. Body squaring keeps the body facing the opponent in the most stable position due to the anchoring of the body by the shoulders and hips perpendicular to the opponent's weaker position.

Fourthly, keeping the body square avoids exposing the body's sides and back unnecessarily. Thus one is less vulnerable to being turned around to expose one's blind spot and vulnerable weak spots such as the kidneys to the opponent's attacks.

2.5 Simultaneous Defence & Attack

A unique characteristic of the martial art of Wing Chun is the principle of Lin Siu Dai Da (loosely translated as Simultaneous Defence & Attack).

Lin Siu Dai Da, Dap Sao and Punch are used at the same time.

The idea of Lin Siu Dai Da postulates that any defensive action must be quickly followed up by an attack in order not to loose the momentary advantage accorded by the opponent. In other words a good defence is a good attack.

The reason for this rationale is that there is a time lag between recognising an attack and coming up with an appropriate defensive response. As reaction time does not favor countering nor blocking, this is clearly a disadvantage to the person being attacked.

Once an attack commences and is allowed to continue the defender will be struck eventually even if he can successfully stop the first few blows. Clearly the odds does not favor the defender being able to stop every punch that is being thrown at him over the long time period.

Lin Siu Dai Da allows the Wing Chun practitioner to turn the table on the attacker and bring the fight back to the attacker.

When used together with the principle of Body Squaring, Lin Siu Dai Da contributes to more efficient use of body resources. Both principles allow the Wing Chun practitioner to always have two hands available for attack and defence. A trained Wing Chun practitioner is like a gunslinger of the old West with two trained guns instead of one.

Combat involves many external factors ranging from positioning, and timing to favorable changes in tactics. The ability to quickly take advantage of momentary openings in the opponent's guard must be there before the opponent is aware of the gap and closes it. Otherwise the conflict will prolong unnecessarily at the expense of sapping one's stamina, concentration and will to win. For this reason the principle of Lin Siu Dai Da gives the Wing Chun practitioner an edge over an opponent who blocks first and punches later.

Unlike the traditional boxing forms of Chinese martial arts that train practitioners the application of different techniques under different situations, the boxing forms of Wing Chun system train practitioners to use different defending and attacking techniques. Actual application of techniques is dependant on the individual practitioner's preference and the situation prevailing. Broadly speaking, Wing Chun's hand techniques are contained in the 3 boxing forms which is classified in the table below:

	Siu Nim Tao		Chum Kiu		Biu Jee	
	Defending	Attacking	Defending	Attacking	Defending	Attacking
	Tan Sao	Straight Punch	Chuen Kiu	Pai Jarn	Biu Sao	Finger Jab
	Jut Sao	Chung Jeung	Dap Sao	Chau Kuen	Jarn Jum Sao	Gwai Jarn
	Wu Sao	Fak Sao	Lan Sao			Chap Kuen
Single hand	Fook Sao	Ding Sao	Jum Sao			
	Pak Sao	High Side Palm	Low Bong Sao			
	Lap Sao	Low Side Palm	Gum Sao			
	Gaun Sao	Reverse Palm				
	Kao Sao					
	High Bong Sao					

	Siu Nim Tao		Chum Kiu		Biu Jee	
	Defending	Attacking	Defending	Attacking	Defending	Attacking
	Double Lan Sao	Double Biu Sao	Double Chuen Kiu	Double Chung Jeung	Man Sao	Horizontal Lap Sao
Double hand	Double Jum Sao	Double Ding Sao	Double Dap Sao		High-low Gaun Sao	
	Double Jut Sao		Double Lap Sao			
	Double Tan Sao		Bong Wu Sao			
	Double Gum Sao		Double Low Bong Sao			

Aside from the double hand techniques, theoretically the principle of simultaneous defence and attack is actually the combination of single hand defending and attacking techniques. Added to this, since the single hand techniques can be used either in left or right hand, the total number of combinations can be calculated by the following formula:

Total No. of Combination of Defending and Attacking Techniques = 4XY

While   X = Defending Techniques
          Y = Attacking Techniques

Put the number of single hand techniques from the above table into this formula (X=17; Y=12), the total no. of combination is 816.

| 1. Jut Sao-High Side Palm | 2. Lap Sao-Fak Sao | 3. Dap Sao-Straight Punch |

2.6 Stances

In traditional Chinese martial arts, a lot of stress is placed on stance training. In the course of combat the body will be subjected to external shocks as a result of the opponent's techniques. Hence if one's body structure is not properly set up and aligned, one will not be able to intercept and neutralize the opponent's powerful techniques.

2.6.1 Yee Jee Kim Yeung Ma

In Wing Chun the fundamental stance is called Yee Jee Kim Yeung Ma which can be translated as "Character Two Goat Adduction Stance".

Yee Jee Kim Yeung Ma plays a key role in teaching the learner the importance of keeping the body square in order to maintain a balanced centreline positioning for the hands.

Forming the Yee Jee Kim Yeung Ma
The following are guidelines to forming the Yee Jee Kim Yeung Ma:
- Stand straight and hold both fists by the side of the body;
- Then bend the knees, open the feet, and turn the feet a little inward such that the toes point towards a common reference point in front – this will cause the legs to be adducted;
- The pelvis is rolled under with the hips pushed up slightly to lengthen out the spine and the waist is kept tucked to unify the upper and lower body;
- Allow the body weight to sink downward through the knees;
- Keep the knees distance around the width of the shoulder;
- Ensure that the back is kept straight;

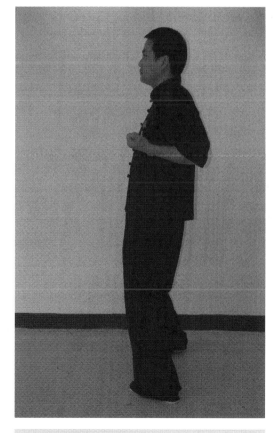

| 1. Front View Yee Jee Kim Yeung Ma | 2. Side View YJKYM |

- Relax the shoulders and chest;
- Keep the head up;
- Let the tongue touch the upper palate gently.

A correctly formed Yee Jee Kim Yeung Ma provides for a stable pyramidal base from which all attack and defense motions originate.

2.6.2 Pien Sun Ma (Side Stance)

The Pien Sun Ma is a side facing stance that is derived from Yee Jee Kim Yeung Ma by turning the body 45° whilst maintaining the square-ness of the body position. The body weight is distributed fully on the leg that the body is positioned over. The other leg lightly touches the ground in readiness to kick or change position.

Neutralizing Path

A very important principle associated with the use of Pien Sun Ma is that of force neutralization. When turning the body from Yee Jee Kim Yeung Ma into Pien Sun Ma the vertical centreline shifts from its original position such that the shoulder now becomes the point to align with the opponent's attacking hand.

Pien Sun Ma with Bong Sao by Chow Sifu

attacking force to emptiness

➤   Leading opponent's force vector to our shoulder

Front arm range

Shoulder Path

Attack

This alignment of the shoulder (hereafter referred to as shoulder path) to that of the opponent's centreline allows for the opponent's powerful force to be neutralized effortlessly by making it fall into emptiness. A direct clashing of opponent's attack from which only the more powerful can prevail is thus avoided.

2.6.3 Ching Sun Ma

The Ching Sun Ma is a frontal facing stance formed by moving the leg from its original position in the Yee Jee Kim Yeung Ma and placing it forward on the centerline. Like the Pien Sun Ma, the Ching Sun Ma also requires the maintaining of the squareness of the body position and the body weight is distributed fully on the rear leg. The leading leg lightly touches the ground in readiness to kick or change position.

Ching Sun Ma with Lan Sao by Chow Sifu

Mobility

The Ching Sun Ma is used for advancing during the application of Wing Chun techniques. The hips are kept facing the front squarely so that the ability to use both hands are maintained. The Ching Sun Ma is a relatively more offensive stance.

Mass Transference

The Ching Sun Ma also allows for the mobilizing of the entire body mass to assist the process of striking. The use of waist springing and weight shifting enables the entire body weight to be projected fully to strike the opponent.

2.6.4 Stance Changing

In our Wing Chun lineage as taught by Grandmaster Yip Man to Chow Tze Chuen Sifu, we are taught to train the Pien Sun Ma and Ching Sun Ma in the Chum Kiu form with 100% of the body weight distributed on the rear leg (hereafter referred as Hau Ma (Rear Stance)). The Hau Ma has the following advantages and disadvantages:

Advantages:
- one can shift the head out of danger;
- make "shadow-less" / invisible kicks easier;
- counter sweep kicks more efficiently;
- easier to absorb / deflect an external force;
- more agile in footwork.

Disadvantages:
- the stance is not very stable;
- follow up techniques are less powerful;
- the reach of arm is reduced.

Biu Bo on Ching Sun Ma with Double Low Bong Sao by Chow Sifu

Despite the disadvantages, the Hau Ma training is still preferred because of the following reasons:

1. To preserve the characteristics / uniqueness of our Wing Chun lineage as originally taught by Grandmaster Yip Man;

2. Hau Ma calls for a more challenging and difficult training in the sense that one must be sensitive to keeping the body consolidated yet precisely positioned so that the body is still relatively stable and not prone to unbalance. But the trainee must still be able to step freely when required to. Once one manages to keep the balance and stability despite using one leg, performing the stance with any weight distribution combination between the two legs should not pose a problem.

3. In our lineage one can compensate for this perceived disadvantage of having less stability by undergoing very hard training to master the single leg balance yet maintain relaxation in the shoulders, elbows, wrists, waist and knees. To overcome the disadvantage of lesser power and reach, the waist is utilized to launch the strikes.

4. It should be noted that since Pien Sun Ma and Ching Sun Ma originated from Yee Jee Kim Yeung Ma, all three stances can change from one to the other easily. During an actual combat situation, one can freely use any appropriate weight distribution in these stances to achieve the objective.

Chapter 3
Neutralizing with Structure

3.1 Importance of Good Structure

In this chapter we discuss one of the essential aspects of the study of martial arts i.e. the study of body structure - its function, practice and application - in relation to the principles and strategies of the martial art of Wing Chun.

The study of body structure is integral to the learning of Wing Chun and calls for a relearning of personal habits that are taken for granted. Good body structure does make a difference to improving one's martial arts skills as discussed in Section 3.2.

3.2 Structure & Combat Strategy

In combat a few primary strategies are necessary to ensure a high probability of success during the course of physical conflict.

Good body structure provides the key to enable these strategies to be realized and functional. These strategies require the Wing Chun practitioner to be able to:

1. Strike the opponent powerfully, quickly and safely without compromising one's safety
2. Be positioned strategically to the opponent's position to fulfil point 1
3. Neutralize a counter-attack with the least effort and return the attack swiftly in conformance with points 1 & 2.
4. Utilize the hands and leg to strike efficiently either independently or simultaneously
5. Mobilize the body to close the gap to strike in keeping with point 1 - 3.

During combat one must address the question of what, how, where and why in relation to the issues of attack, defence and counter-attack. The Wing Chun practitioner should understand the implications of different types of techniques and strategies, and the external factors governing pugilism such as distance, timing, speed, mass, force and change to maximize his success rate in an encounter.

The Wing Chun body structure is configured to enable the Wing Chun practitioner to maximize his strong points while minimizing his risk exposure.

In this respect the Wing Chun fighter should consider that as fast as he can move, the opponent could be just as fast or faster. The opponent may also be heavier, taller and have longer reach; and the range at which one can hit the opponent is also the range at which the opponent can hit back.

Adherence to the fundamental Wing Chun principles as outlined in Chapter 2 plus a good body structure can enable one to handle an opponent with superior speed, mass, height and reach. Distancing can also be addressed by either entering from the opponent's blind side, unbalancing the opponent through displacement or sealing the opponent's limbs as one is closing in the distance to strike. The companion videotape illustrates these points in greater detail.

In Chow Sifu's lineage of Wing Chun as transmitted by Grandmaster Yip Man, good body structure calls for:

- *static elbow positioning*
- *the use of the triangulation body structure*
- *the single weighted leg distribution*
- *waist springing*

The illustration of Points 2 and 3 is shown in the photos in Section 2.6.3 of Chapter 2. Please note though Chow Sifu's stance is slanted backwards he is not leaning backward while the entire body weight is placed on the rear leg. In the next section we will discuss the practice of good body structure.

3.3 Developing Good Structure

In Wing Chun, the training of the body weapon starts on day one when the fundamental form, Siu Nim Tao, is learned.

The Siu Nim Tao form drills the practitioner in the different aspects of cultivating good body structure. Study themes such as the following are covered :-

- *keeping a centered upright posture*
- *maintaining stable balance through phasic knee bends*
- *unifying the upper and lower body through waist force*
- *understanding the use of joints*
- *creating a force vector path through body linkage and alignment*
- *manipulating the hands for attack and defence in line with triangular path*
- *having a flexible yet strong arm bridge based on alignment and structure*

The subject of Siu Nim Tao will be covered in a future volume. In this volume we will confine ourselves to covering the fundamentals of our Wing Chun system.

Below we discuss the anatomical parts of the body involved in the setting up of good body structure. They are:

Head

The head should be kept upright and the neck comfortably straightened; correct alignment uplifts the body by lengthening the spinal process and keeps one well balanced and agile.

Shoulders

The shoulders should be dropped to eliminate unnecessary tension caused by the shoulder muscles. Eliminating this unwanted tension improves the release of power through articulation of the striking arm through flexion and extension.

Elbows

The elbows should be kept lowered in front of the body to protect the body. Other benefits of aligning the body behind the arms include :

•   convergent alignment of the hands with the centerline rather than divergence as mentioned in Section 2.1 in Chapter 2. This also reduces the tendency to resist against the opponent's hand techniques.

•   additional protection for the body; one can likened it to the secondary gate of a house which acts as a last resort to protect the body should the opponent's attack penetrates past one's front gate parameter as defined at the wrist of an extended guarding arm.

•   immovable elbow positioning as elaborated in Section 2.3 of Chapter 2.

•   provide a focal point for all techniques to originate from the body's physical centerline in accordance to the maxim "Man Fat Gwai Chung" (translated as "ten thousand techniques originate from the centerline") – this provides a measure of defence when attacking and positions the entire body mass behind the hands.

Wrist

The wrists should be gently locked upon impact to impart a sudden impulse force to magnify the initial force generated by the body. Spiral force can be added by twisting the wrist before impact. The wrists also act as the first portal to receive the opponent's attack.

Chest

The chest should be raised but not thrown out nor depressed; the reduction in tension from a hunched or compressed chest facilitates natural breathing.

Back

The back should be kept straightened such that the head, tailbone and rear heel is aligned in a straight line. By so doing the center of gravity can be easily positioned over one leg when changing from Yee Jee Kim Yeung Ma to Pien Sun Ma or Ching Sun Ma.

Waist

The waist is to be kept depressed down gently so that the body does not have tendency to tilt backwards or lean forward. This is referred to as keeping the force in the waist and is an essential component to the process of using the waist to generate force or absorbing force.

Pelvis

The pelvis should be gently raised and thrust forward. This enables the body's center of gravity to be balanced such that kicks can be delivered without having to move the body weight about unnecessarily and thus telegraph the body's intention to launch a kicking attack. Tilting the pelvis gives the Wing Chun practitioner the characteristic triangulation body structure.

Thighs

The thighs should be adducted rather than forcing the knees to come together. This allows the body's resources to converge towards a common sagittal plane; allowing body mass to be linked as and when required. The thighs can also assist in the process of neutralization together with the waist swallowing.

Feet

The feet should be pointed forward to the imaginary apex of a triangle. The hip joints must be kept relaxed so that the legs can move freely.

To be able to move swiftly, the body must be kept vertical in conformance to points (a) to (j) at all times. Locomotion is the province of the waist force and feet. Power is governed by the waist, legs and back.

We can say that generally major joints such as the shoulder, elbow, wrist, waist, kua, knees and ankles must maintain a constant state of relaxation. Under this condition the joints can move freely and absorb force; circling can also be utilized to yield and move around any rigid resistance offered by the opponent.

The importance of correct body alignment is stated in the Wing Chun maxim which goes "Yiu Ma Hup Yat; Dao Sao Hup Yat" (waist horse unite as one; knives hands unite as one).

3.4 Neutralizing with Structure

In Wing Chun there is a maxim "Ying Siu Bo Fa" which means "Structure Neutralizes, Footwork Dissolves". From this we can see the importance placed by our Wing Chun ancestors on good body structure.

From the point of view of combat, good structure:

1. Enables the Wing Chun practitioner to withstand, absorb and deflect external shocks resulting from the opponent's forceful attack without resorting to using one's brute strength to resist against the opponent's strength. The following Sections 3.5 and 3.6 will elaborate more on this point.
2. Facilitates the issuance of power from the ground through the heels to the hand
3. Allows the body to move and step swiftly yet maintain sound balance
4. Keep the integrity of the body posture such that the opponent is unable to borrow the Wing Chun practitioner's strength and exploit it to his advantage

3.5 Yielding Like Willow

In Chapter 1 the metaphor of the willow tree was introduced. In general we can liken the hands of the Wing Chun practitioner to the branches of the willow tree that give way in the onslaught of a stronger opponent without violating the integrity of the centreline.

The famed Wing Chun master Leung Jan was said to have taught his disciples to play the pipa before even starting their Wing Chun training to enable them to first loosen their wrists. From this we can see how important relaxation is if the Wing Chun practitioner is to be able to use a soft approach to prevail over a strong opponent.

However it is not only the hands alone that are involved in the neutralization and absorbing of the opponent's force. An upright and aligned body also plays an important role to assist to receive the opponent's force and redirect it into the ground harmlessly by using the waist and legs as stated by the maxim "Loi Lau Hui Sung" (Retain What Comes, Escort What Goes).

In addition the development of strong and stable stance allows the Wing Chun practitioner's body to be stable and not easily susceptible to an external force when coming into contact with the opponent.

3.6 Leading to Emptiness with Shoulder Path

This is the foremost mechanism for yielding to a stronger force in Wing Chun. This key idea calls for the Wing Chun practitioner to lead the opponent's force to fall into emptiness by using the shoulder path.

The principle of using the shoulder path can be applied whether the Wing Chun practitioner is:

- *remaining static while occupying the centre*
- *pivoting or turning the body*
- *stepping*

In Section 2.4 we introduced the use of a simple two-dimensional equilateral triangle to reference one's centre to the opponent for the purpose of attack and defence. The two sides of this triangle define the path to lead the opponent's movements to fall into emptiness.

The first section of Chum Kiu best illustrates the practice of using the shoulder path on turning the body while performing a Bong Sao. In this exercise as illustrated in the photo the following pointers must be observed:

1. The body stops turning when the Bong Sao is directly aligned to the shoulder
2. The body is removed from the line of attack by shifting the entire body weight onto the rear leg.
3. The body must be kept square on to the line of attack in order to maintain the shape of the equilateral triangle so that both hands can be used for attack and defence

Pivoting with Bong Sao in Chum Kiu

3.7 Structure & Footwork

The maxim "Ying Siu Bo Fa" points out that in learning and application of body structure should come first.

An objective of Wing Chun is the minimal use of the body to overcome the opponent commonly referred to as using "stillness to overcome motion" in the practice of Chinese martial arts. This implies that if the Wing Chun practitioner can control the opponent with his body structure while remaining in the same spot either by using his waist to effect a superior distance or pivoting to create a shoulder path, that would be ideal.

However the dynamics of an actual conflict is such that sometimes it is not possible to just rely on body structure while standing rooted to the same spot. A swift moving opponent who can move in quickly or a powerful and massive opponent may neutralize the advantages of good body structure.

Under such circumstances the use of footwork is called for hence the phrase "Bo Fa" in the second part of the maxim "Ying Siu Bo Fa" which implies that when body structure is not sufficient footwork must come into play.

In Chapter 4 – Dissolving Using Footwork, we will go into greater detail on the use of footwork in Wing Chun.

Chapter 4
Dissolving Using Footwork

4.1 Role of Footwork

In Wing Chun an important idea is to be able to control an opponent using the body structure. This is primarily cultivated at the Siu Nim Tao level. However if the opponent's force is stronger than what one's static structure is able to absorb then it is neutralized by using body turning with the body weight distributed 100% on the rear leg coupled with the shoulder path alignment while the central axis remains upright. This is trained in the first section of Chum Kiu. The concept of using structure to neutralize has been explained earlier in Chapter 3.

Against an exceptionally strong opponent body turning alone may not suffice. This is where footwork comes into play to remove one's body totally from the path of the force or by following the direction of the force vector.

A secondary purpose of footwork is to always maintain an ideal range between oneself and the opponent to safely defend and counterattack in whichever direction the opponent choses to move.

Another role for footwork is to adjust ones centerline to face the opponent properly.

4.2 Type of Footwork

In our Wing Chun approach we basically have three important ways to mobilize the body:

- *Tor Bo*
- *Biu Bo*
- *Huen Bo*

Tor Bo by front leg

Tor Bo is the sideward movement of the body sitting on Pien Sun Ma by using the front leg.

Photos Explanation: Tor Bo by front leg / Body turning & Shoulder path / Application of Gum Sao, low Bong Sao and Lap Sao-Fak Sao

S : Sifu Donald Mak on the right side
O : Opponent on the left side

S and O both at ready position, S Bai-jong with Bong-Wu Sao sitting on the Pien Sun Ma

O advances and attacks S with a punch;
S Tor Bo by using the front leg to shift to his left side in order to move his body from the path of the force.

S shifts himself to the right side of O and blocks O's punch by the Gum Sao coupled with the shoulder path alignment

O withdraws his right punch and launch the left punch to S

S uses the right low Bong Sao to defend

6 – 8 S changes his Wu Sao (left) - low Bonq Sao (right) to Lap Sao (left) – Fak Sao (right) on O's neck

Tor Bo by rear leg

Photos Explanation: Tor Bo by rear leg
Shoulder path / Concurrent striking and kicking / Application of Knee-Stamping Kick

S : Sifu Donald Mak on the left side
O : Opponent on the right side

S and O both at ready position, S Bai-jong with Bong-Wu Sao sitting on the Pien Sun Ma

S Tor Bo by using the rear leg to shift to his left side in order to move his body from the path of the force.

O advances and attacks S with a right tiger claw (Fu-jow).

S shifts himself to the right side of O coupled with the shoulder path alignment and simultaneously covers himself with a left Wu Sao and right low Gang Sao.

S changes his low Gang Sao (right) – Wu Sao (left) to Lap Sao (right) – Punch (left) and raise his right leg ready for the concurrent strike and kick.

S then launch a Lap Sao-punch (Lap on O's right hand) and thrusts out his right leg in a slant-straight forward line to stamp at O's right knee.

Biu Bo as its name implies is the method of moving the body forward quickly while sitting on Ching Sun Ma. Biu Bo relies on the waist to propel the entire body forward as one unit. By moving the whole body concurrently the entire body mass is mobilized thereby maximizing bodily momentum behind a strike.

Biu Bo

Photos Explanation: Tor Bo by front leg / Triangular Footwork – Basic and Biu Bo / Shoulder path / Simultaneous Block & Strike / Application of Dap Sao

S : Sifu Donald Mak on the right side
O : Opponent on the left side

S and O both at ready position, S Bai-jong, places his right hand in front of his left hand sitting on the Pien Sun Ma.

O advances and attacks S with a Kup Chui; S Tor Bo by using the front leg to shift to his left side in order to move his body from the path of the force.

17 – 18 S shifts himself to the right side of O by Huen Bo and Biu Bo (triangular footwork – Basic) to block O's punch by Dap Sao coupled with the shoulder path alignment

19 – 20 Simultaneously S punches on O's rib cage.

Huen Bo is stepping using the leading leg to describe a semi-circle on the ground in the process of moving forward. Tracing the semi-circle has a number of functions as follows:

• Protect the groin by using the thigh to shield the groin from a kick aimed at the groin as one is charging forward to close the gap. Since the groin is a fragile organ which cannot take a blow, it must be well protected as a blow would certainly mean defeat.

• Avoid clashing with the opponent's front leg especially if the opponent is in a bow and arrow stance by circling around the opponent's leg and then lightly adhering to his leg to control it.

• Sweep the opponent's leg thus unbalancing the opponent, making it easier to counterattack the opponent.

Huen Bo

Photos Explanation: Triangular Footwork – Complex / Shoulder path / Concurrent strike and kick / Application of Back-Sweep Leg

S : Sifu Donald Mak on the right side
O : Opponent on the left side

S and O both at ready position, S Bai-jong, places his right hand in front of his left hand sitting on the Ching Sun Ma

22 – 23 O advances and attacks S with his right punch moving upward to groin. S withdraws his left leg back by Huen Bo to shift to his left side in order to move his body from the path of the force.

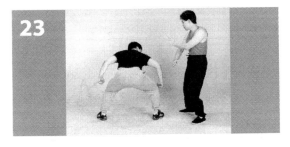

24 – 25 S immediately advances with the Huen Bo coupled with the shoulder path alignment to O's right side and uses the Back-Sweep leg and Pak Sao-High side palm concurrently.

Aside from moving forward only, the leading leg can also be drawn sideways in an arc in preparation for the other leg to be mobilized forward to replace the withdrawn leg.

Huen Bo back

Photos Explanation: Biu Bo / Huen Bo back / Use of waist / Application of High & Low Gang Sao; Jut Sao-High side palm

S : Sifu Donald Mak on the left side
O : Opponent on the right side

S and O both at ready position, S Bai-jong, places his right hand in front of his left hand sitting on the Ching Sun Ma

27 – 28 S advances with the left leg Biu Bo and attacks O with a right punch

O blocks and attacks S simultaneously.

30 – 31 S withdraws his left leg back by Huen Bo and turns to use the high & low Gang Sao to block O's left punch and right blocking arm.

32-33 S changes his high Gang Sao (left) to left Jut Sao (right) pressing heavily on O's right blocking arm while quickly springs his waist to thrust the right high side palm to O's neck.

Wing Chun footwork training involves playing with the three fundamental footwork within a number of prearranged patterns as described below in 4.5. These exercises are invaluable to understanding the core ideas underlying the strategy of a willow tree bending in the face of a strong wind as a metaphor for using a soft approach to handle a strong external force.

4.3 Footwork in Forms

In Wing Chun, footwork is normally introduced formally at the Chum Kiu level.

In Chum Kiu, the idea of using Tor Bo and Biu Bo are covered in the second and third section of the form. Huen Bo is introduced in Biu Jee. At the wooden dummy level both footwork patterns are drilled within the framework of attack and defence.

Footwork must always be practiced together with the principles of the shoulder path, maintaining the ability to strike with the hands and legs at the same time and using the stepping to aid the body structure to neutralize a very powerful force. These ideas are again reemphasized when drilling the wooden dummy to fine tune the precision demanded of the principles. Future volumes on the Chum Kiu and Wooden Dummy forms will go into detail of how the principles are practiced within each section of the forms.

Footwork in Wooden Dummy Form – From Bong Sao to Tan-da

The most advanced footwork is found in the Bart Jarm Dao knives form. If the Wing Chun practitioner is restricted to using a weight distribution of 100:0 earlier, the Bart Jarm Dao training strives to free the practitioner from this constraint by training him to freely utilize the entire range of weight distribution from a totally weighted rear leg to loading the weight on the front leg during striking throughout a variable range of weighting during the transient stage of a technique.

Footwork in Knives Form – From trapping knives to chasing chop

According to Chow Sifu, Grandmaster Yip Man once mentioned that a strike is more powerful and hence difficult to stop if the strike is executed with the weight forward. Grandmaster Yip Man further said that using knives for self-defence in a modern society was no longer practical and hence knife training is for the purpose of enhancing one's empty hand skills especially the footwork rather than an end by itself.

4.4 Soft Approach & Footwork

As explained above, a simple but comprehensive pattern of footwork underlies the Wing Chun system. This is in keeping with the principle of "Ying Siu Bo Fa" which translates as "Structure Neutralizes, Footwork Dissolves".

The introduction of footwork expands the range of movements available to the Wing Chun practitioner to not only neutralize but close the gap, chase, adhere, stick and follow the opponent's movements in all directions. At the same time the opponent constantly finds his movements cut off, restricted or falls on empty space without having the opportunity to use his strength to strike back at the Wing Chun practitioner.

Using of footwork *(Tor Bo by rear leg, Huen Bo back, Huen Bo and Biu Bo) to close the gap, chase, adhere stick and follow the opponent's movements in all directions*

Photos Explanation: Tor Bo by rear leg / Triangular Footwork – Complex and Biu Bo / Shoulder path / Application of Low Bong Sao; Gum Sao-High side palm

S : Sifu Donald Mak on the left side
O : Opponent on the right side

S and O both at ready position, S Bai-jong, places his right hand in front of his left hand sitting on the Ching Sun Ma

O advances and attacks S with a left uppercut.

S Tor Bo by using the rear leg to shift to his right side in order to move his body from the path of the force and use the right Low Bong Sao to deflect O's uppercut.

44 – 47 O continues to attack S with the right hook punch. S withdraws his left leg back by Huen Bo and turns to use the left Gum Sao to follow O's downward movement by pressing O's right arm while S advances with the Huen Bo-Biu Bo to adhere.

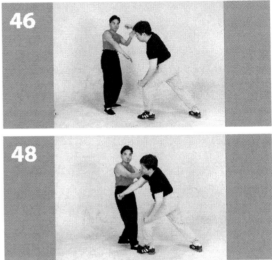

48 – 49 S uses the left Gum Sao pressing heavily on O's right arm while quickly springs his waist to thrust the right high side palm to O's neck.

4.5 Practice of Footwork

Apart from the footwork training in Wing Chun Forms mentioned above, basic stepping exercises for training the ability to use the Tor Bo, Biu Bo and Huen Bo can be further practiced with the Triangular Footwork (Sam Kok Bo). Triangular Footwork has two stepping patterns namely, i) basic pattern and ii) complex pattern.

Mui Faa Stake Stepping (Mui Faa Zong) is a unique training method of footwork in Wing Chun. Mui Faa means plum flower. Its name comes from the configuration of the posts, which, when viewed from above, resembles a plum flower. Practice on Mui Faa stakes can have the following benefits:

- Strengthen the footwork
- Concept and application of Ying/Yang, Sinking/Rising
- Stepping on the five Mui Faa points towards your opponents in different directions
- Special stepping footwork (Step back but not retreating backwards, while having a rooted stance to "generate your force from the ground")
- Solo leg standing posture for balance
- Combination of techniques
- Front and Side body facing method

Mui Faa Jong

51-55 Movements on Mui Faa Jong

Chapter 5
Shadowless Kicks

5.1 Misconception on Wing Chun Kicks Dispelled

Ever since Wing Chun exploded into public consciousness the perception has long been held that Wing Chun is a martial art that predominantly relies only on fast short range hand techniques.

Nothing could be further from the truth. The late Grandmaster Yip Man once said (as quoted in the book "Wing Chun" by Yip Chun and Michael Tze):

"In Wing Chun, we actually train our legs twice as hard as we train our hands. There is a saying in the martial arts : "the hands are like swing doors, defence is in the legs". That means the hands are for opening, entering, contacting, distracting and controlling - the real defence is found in the legs, in your balance and your powerful leg attacks" From Grandmaster Yip's insightful comment we can see that there is a special place in Wing Chun for the use of the legs and this role is not any lesser than that of the hands. The skilful control of the legs give rise to the following benefits :

1. Dynamic balance
2. Lively footwork
3. Shadowless kicks

In Chapters 2 and 4 we have outlined the role of Wing Chun stances and footwork. In this chapter we touch on another additional benefit of being able to use Wing Chun's 100:0 weighted stances i.e. the ability to unleash non-telegraphic kicks suddenly while eliminating all other unnecessary movements to rebalance the body in a position that facilitates kicking.

In short the Wing Chun practitioner should retain the ability to strike with any hand and leg as desired at any time. With this the Wing Chun man effectively has 3 hands for the purpose of attacking, defending and counterattacking.

5.2 What is Wing Chun Kicking Skill?

The use of leg techniques, which is also known as kicking attacks or kicking techniques, is our Chinese martial arts' expression of the skills of the lower limbs in the art of self defense. In Chow Sifu's early days of learning under Grandmaster Yip Man, he was advised repeatedly that since he is short in stature and size (Chow Sifu is about 5' 2" in height), he should emphasize the training of the lower body (the training of the lower body covers the stances, waist usage, footwork and kicking techniques). There is a saying in Chinese martial arts training that is 'in order to succeed, you have to be diligent enough and also able to endure hardship'.

The late Grandmaster Yip Man's specialty skill in Wing Chun is that of kicking techniques. This was Grandmaster Yip's most commonly used skill in overcoming an opponent. During the time when Grandmaster Yip was the group leader of a secret investigation team in Fatshan, he already had the reputation of being able to break three wooden poles with one kick.

In another incident which occurred after Grandmaster Yip had migrated to Hong Kong in 1949, there was this incident whereby a strong young ruffian was defeated with a single kicking technique.

This incident happened in the days when Hong Kong was still an undeveloped city. Grandmaster Yip was staying in an area with extremely poor living conditions. The living conditions were so terrible that there was no pipe-in water and families had to retrieve water from a public tap by the roadside. There was an incident once whereby Grandmaster Yip was standing in the queue waiting for his turn to fill his bucket with water. Suddenly there was this young muscular chap who thinking that he would use his brawn to get his way decided to cut into the queue.

Seeing this ruffian take undue advantage of the situation Grandmaster Yip went up to him to have a word with him on his unreasonable behavior since everyone else was queuing for their turn. However the young ruffian not only did not want to listen, he decided to teach Grandmaster Yip a lesson.

In that split second before the ruffian's blow could land, Grandmaster Yip had already used his Chuen Kiu (a movement from Chum Kiu) hand technique to intercept the blow and simultaneously used a front kick to drop the ruffian. This incident illustrates the depth of Grandmaster Yip Man's skill in the Wing Chun leg techniques.

Although Chow Sifu heard of the above incident through hearsay, during the course of Grandmaster Yip's teaching, there was once where he demonstrated this technique to Chow Sifu and it left a vivid impression because of its realistic simulation. Especially memorable is Grandmaster Yip's demonstration of Kwan Sao with a kick.

Quick as a bolt of lighting Grandmaster Yip was able to simultaneously strike with his kick and neutralize with his hands without having to extricate his kicking leg first in preparation or moving his body. Grandmaster Yip's fierce kick came through so quickly to Chow Sifu's stomach that Chow Sifu was not able to stop it yet Grandmaster Yip's control was so good that he only touched Chow Sifu gently without injuring him. Grandmaster Yip's precise and nimble control of his kicking power enabled him to demonstrate to Chow Sifu this aspect of the Wing Chun skills.

Another time Grandmaster Yip was demonstrating how to use one's leg as though it was a hand. He instructed Chow Sifu to extend the Tan Sao posture and then Grandmaster Yip used the Fook Gerk to place on Chow Sifu's Tan Sao. Thereafter Grandmaster Yip with a downward retracting motion was able to pull Chow Sifu off-balance and further caused him to bend his knees and fall to the ground. This was Chow Sifu's personal experience of Grandmaster Yip's maxim of using the leg as if using a hand.

Grandmaster Yip's total confidence in the use of Wing Chun's leg techniques can be seen in another incident. During the early days when Wing Chun was gaining a foothold in Hong Kong, it was common for other martial arts styles to come to try out the new kid on the block by holding a competition whether by invitation or direct challenge.

During this time, another southern Chinese style that was renowned for their use of footwork and whirling hand techniques wanted to test out Grandmaster Yip's Wing Chun school and a competition was organized accordingly.

However Grandmaster Yip would only agree to the competition readily on condition that kicking techniques could also be used. Unfortunately the competition was called off in the end for some unknown reason. Notwithstanding the cancellation of the competition, this reflected Grandmaster Yip's confidence in Wing Chun kicking techniques.

5.3 Why Use Kicks?
There is a saying in Chinese martial arts that goes "Nam Kuen, Pak Tuei" (translated as Southern Fists, Northern Kicks). This is a commonly heard saying in Chinese martial arts circle to mean that southern Chinese martial arts are famed for the use of the hands whereas northern Chinese martial arts are well versed in the use of the legs.

Wing Chun is a southern Chinese system of martial arts that is well known for skillful use of the hands which alone is sufficient to overcome an opponent. From this a misunderstanding has arisen that Wing Chun is lacking in kicking skills and its kicks are lacking as compared to the more well known northern Chinese styles which specializes in this area.

Moreover it is popularly held that it is safer to use the hands during combat in which techniques are being exchanged very fast. The common belief is that if one's leg is off the ground even for a split second one is then momentarily unbalanced and this could be exploited by the opponent. This could possibly be the main reason why so few kicks are observed and actually used in the majority of southern style Chinese martial arts.

In the attack and defense skills of Wing Chun, kicking belongs to a higher level of skill cultivation due to the higher demands on body control that is required in order to be able to apply this skill freely. The use of kicking techniques should also be in combination with the principles of centerline control and concurrent striking and defense.

As observed by Grandmaster Yip (as mentioned in Section 5.1) the use of leg techniques can accord a good winning edge in the sense that the hands are akin to two swinging doors that opens up the opponent to be destroyed with the devastating kicks. Furthermore there is a boxing proverb that says the fists strikes 30% of the time whereas the kicks are used during the remaining 70%.

In furtherance to the above we can classify the role and purpose of Wing Chun leg techniques into three categories:

Pak/Tan-Slanting Kick

1. Using the weak to overcome the strong. The legs are naturally longer and also stronger than the hands. This gives an advantage to the user of kicks in overcoming an opponent. The use of kicks is especially suited for those of small stature and consequently have problems overcoming a much bigger and taller person due to height and length disparity of the arms. As a martial art that stresses the principle of economy of motion, Wing Chun kicks do not go above the height of the waist. Thus kicks that require shifting, jumping and leaping are not used in Wing Chun.

2. Ability to deliver an unexpected attack on the opponent. The Wing Chun practitioner can coordinate the use of his two hands to strike together with his leg techniques within the distance of a single arm bridge to defeat the opponent. This requires the use of the hands to

Using a kick to neutralize a kick

Stop Kick

Fook Gerk

Fook Gerk & Stop Kick to neutralize a kick

distract the opponent while adjusting the lower limbs to strike without alerting the opponent. This is in line with the famous Chinese 36 Strategies of "feint to the east, attack to the west" to steal the thunder on the opponent.

3. Using a kick to neutralize a kick. The Wing Chun practitioner who is using kicks for attack and defense must take note that the upper and middle body zone is the province of the hands with the legs used in the lower body zone to counterattack. When using the legs one must use the legs to neutralize and concurrently in combination with the hands counterattack the opponent's leg attacks to the lower body zone with one's own kicks. Only then can one fulfil the requirement of the Wing Chun maxim "when you want to strike to the top (of the body zone), I strike to the bottom; when you strike to the bottom, I will strike to the top".

5.4 Shadowless Kicking Method

Wing Chun's kicking attack is not only swift and speedy like lightning but precise and unpredictable. Wing Chun's shadowless kick is so called because it is sudden and quick as a flash of lighting; so quick that the opponent does not even have the opportunity to react to the kick. This is how the name and concept of the "Mo Ying Gerk" (the Cantonese term for Shadowless Kick) came about.

The ability to execute a flawless Wing Chun shadowless kick is dependent on the following primary requirements:

1. The attacking motion must be minimal and tight in order to be sudden and non-telegraphic, yet the reach of the kick must be wide and far to retain the power of the movement.

2. Secondly the movements must be linked by maintaining the flexibility of the posture, stances and footwork. This can only be achieved if one is soft and relaxed.

To achieve minimal attacking motion, the following principles must be observed:

1. Motionless Upper Body and No Retraction of Kicking Leg

When one is using kicks the upper body must not move and the kicking leg must be able to kick out straightaway without the need to draw back first. It is common to see martial arts practitioners tilt the body when kicking. Tilting the body may put more mass behind the kicking leg but this is at the expense of physically telegraphing to a

Comparison between a Wing Chun kicking Movement and a non-Wing Chun kicking movement

skiled opponent as to when to expect a kick, rendering the kicking attack easier to counter. The requirement in Wing Chun is that the upper body must remain motionless.

2. Simultaneous Usage of Arms and Legs

Wing Chun's leg techniques maintain that "without hands, there are no legs". This means that if one were to unleash a kick there should be an accompanying

Simultaneous Usage of Arms and Legs

appropriate hand technique. One should never hastily use the kicks on their own. With the accompanying use of the hands one can "feint to the east, attack to the west" to simultaneously attack and defend. Only then can one be assured of victory.

3. Leg Should Not Exceed Waist Height

The kicking leg should never go above the level of one's own waist in order to maintain a tight and closed attack yet keep the body balanced when attacking with a kick. The correct place to attack with the legs will be discussed below.

4. Using the Leg Like a Hand

Grandmaster Yip would constantly admonish Chow Sifu during training sessions that one's legs should be used as if one were using hands. The requirement for using the hands in Wing Chun is that they must be acutely sensitive and agile, able to react at the correct moment, guarding the centerline closely, maintaining a state of natural relaxation, and sink and drop the shoulders. The elbows and shoulder are likened the knees and the kua respectively.

5.5 Principles of Kicking Techniques in Wing Chun

The fundamental principle in using the legs for kicking in Wing Chun is to relax. By relaxing one can then issue natural leg power.

Moreover before executing a kick the Wing Chun practitioner must first relax the waist and kua, and sink the breath to the Dan Tian. Only then will the power reside in the waist and then extend to the knees before reaching the lower thigh and finally reaching the heel. If punching is akin to shooting an arrow, then kicking in Wing Chun is like unleashing a whip.

The use of kicks in Wing Chun also requires that one should be able to retract the kicking leg immediately after kicking to prevent the leg from being grabbed and exposing one to the danger of being thrown to the ground. One's kick should also be able to be drawn back for another follow-up or change in attacking strategy should the kick be intercepted by the opponent.

5.6 The Kicks of Wing Chun

Wing Chun's kicking method is to let the heel do the leading. Within this principle there can be found the method of hooking, stamping, sweeping and flicking. These are the expressions of kicking that can be found in the Wing Chun Wooden Dummy to deal with different situations.

The following are the kicks found in the Wooden Dummy:

Kwan Sao – Side Kick

Tan Da – Slanting Kick to the Knee

Tan Da – Front Kick

Chuen Kiu – Front Kick

Kwan Sao – Trampling Kick
Pak Sao – Detaining Kick

Kwan Sao – Low Side Kick

Pak Sao –Stomp Kick

Gaun Sao – Sweeping Kick

Tok Sao – Front Kick

Tan Da – Low Front Kick
Pak/Tan - Slanting Kick

Lap Da – Slanting Kick

The main target areas for kicking in Wing Chun resides in the body's middle and lower zone. The middle zone includes Dan Tian, tail bone, groin, floating ribs and solar plexus. The bottom zone includes upper inner thighs, knees, ankles, instep, calves and shins.

Below is the classification table of specific targets for Wing Chun kicks:

Kicking Technique	Kicking Method	Kicking Target
Stomp Using the heel to thrust	Kwan Sao – Side Kick Kwan Sao – Low Side Kick	Dan Tian, ribs, groin, knees
	Tan Da – Slanting Kick Pak Sao – Slanting Kick to Knee	Knees
	Tan Da – Front Kick Pak/Tan – Slanting Kick	Solar plexus, Dan Tian, groin
	Chuen Kiu – Front Kick Jut Sao – Front Kick Lap Da – Slanting Kick	Dan Tian, groin, solar plexus
	Tan Da – Low Front Kick	Knees, calves
Hook Using the foot to un-balance and cause the opponent to fall	Pak Da – Detaining Kick	Ankle
Trample Using the entire foot or the bottom of the foot to forcefully stomp the opponent	Kwan Sao – Trampling Kick	Shins, lower thigh, upper inner thigh
Sweep Using the shin to kick the opponent's lower body	Gaun Sao – Sweeping Kick	Calves, ankle
Hook Using the sole or tip to kick the opponent's groin or tailbone	Tan Da – Front Kick Pak/Tan - Slanting Kick	Groin, tailbone

The use of leg to neutralize a kick involves Bong Gerk, Fook Gerk and Jit Gerk (i.e Stop kick).

5.7 Essentials of Leg Training

When using kicks for combat, it is very important to be non-telegraphic, fast and agile. This is because there is a time lag between the time the kicking foot is lifted off the ground to kick and placing it back on to the ground again. This momentary time lag also affects the body's ability to move fast.

Fook Gerk to neutralize a kick

As such, this delay not only gives the opponent a chance to evade the kick but also gives the opponent the opportunity to counter-attack. Therefore before attempting the use of kicking, one should build a good foundation by training the legs first. However before training the legs, one should develop the use of footwork first. The training of footwork is covered in Chapter 4.

In short the Wing Chun practitioner should strive to achieve kicks which are flexible and supple because when one is slow in using kicks to attack then it will be difficult to overcome the opponent. It is only when one has attained the stage of supple and flexibility should one try to achieve a high degree of accuracy.

The ability to kick swiftly depends on a number of factors namely:

1. *stable stance especially during movement*
2. *elusive and unpredictable footwork*
3. *ability to control the facing direction*
4. *distribution of weight placement between the legs smoothly especially on the supporting leg*

Without factors (1) to (4) above one's kicks will be slow and clumsy. Under such circumstances the use of kicks can only endanger oneself and it is better not to use kicking at all.

The training of the legs in Wing Chun starts with the cultivation of a stable static stance in the Siu Nim Tao form. The use of different stances - Side Stance (Pien Sun Ma) and Frontal Stance (Ching Sun Ma), correct way to move the body during turning and stepping, and most importantly the proper placement of the body weight to be entirely on the supporting leg is introduced in the Chum Kiu form. These variables train the Wing Chun practitioner to be stable yet agile, which is the fundamental requirement when learning to kick. The subject of stances is covered in Chapter 2.

The use of somersaults, leaping and jumping in kicking is avoided in Wing Chun's leg techniques. All kicks are aimed only at the middle or lower body zone. When training kicking in Wing Chun there is no need to follow the methods of Chinese northern style kicks; it is sufficient to adhere to Wing Chun's methods which are:

1 Solo leg kicking method
2 Sticking leg (Chi Gerk)
3 Kicking Dummy

1. Solo Leg Kicking Method
All Wing Chun practitioners who take up kicking must first learn to kick smoothly. This in trained in the solo leg kicking method which requires numerous repetitions to master. Without this hard work, the Wing Chun practitioner will not be able to generate power. Different styles have different kicking practices. The following are Wing Chun's solo kicking practice methods:

a. Using the right leg as your center of gravity, stand upright and have the right hand extended in the Biu Jee Sao posture.

b. Then have the left leg face forward and execute a front kick. Kick to the extreme extension of the kicking leg to generate power so that upon conclusion of the kick, the kicking leg will automatically retract back to the original position. Thereafter the retracting leg traces a small circle before executing another front kick.

c. Repeat number (b), there are no limit to the number of times one can do this.

d. Continue to keep the left leg up in the air without touching the ground, turn the body and change into Kwan Sao with Wang Gerk (Side Kick).

e. The right leg continues to stand in an upright posture while supporting the entire body's weight. Then using the whole body as an axle, kick out the right leg once after each turn of the body. Again there are no limits to how many times one can turn in training.

f. Reverse number (a) and (e) for the left and right leg.

g. Note that while practicing kicking, the upper body has to remain still.

2. Sticking Leg (Chi Gerk)
Sticking leg is the second level skill of training in Wing Chun's leg techniques. There are 4 reasons for training the sticking leg:

a. cultivate the balance of the supporting leg
b. training the waist, kua and knee to become supple and smooth
c. train the sensitivity of both legs
d. achieve the stage of using hands and legs interchangeably.

Chi Gerk

3. Kicking Dummy

The Wing Chun Kicking Dummy set contains all the earlier listed kicking techniques in Section 5.6. The Kicking Dummy was extracted and consolidated by Grandmaster Yip from the normal eight section 116 Wooden Dummy set to form a separate dummy form solely for training the kicks. The main purpose of training the Kicking Dummy is to develop the waist, stance, stepping, hand strike and kicking to move as one.

In addition to the above three drills, there are two additional optional drills which were transmitted by Grandmaster Yip Man. One of them was mentioned earlier in Section 5.2 on developing the use of one's leg as though it was a hand involving the use of the trainee's Fook Gerk to move his partner who is in a Tan Sao posture. The second method involves the use of the leg to pull down a rope loop attached to a piece of rattan before kicking the dummy; this develops a stable single legged stance, waist and leg power.

5.8 Summary of Wing Chun Kicking Skill

Wing Chun kicking techniques is a difficult skill to acquire. To be able to kick is easy but to kick within the parameters demanded by Wing Chun principles and strategy as transmitted by Grandmaster Yip Man and outlined in this chapter is another matter.

The ability to use kicking techniques has to be realized in sticking hand before one is able to apply it freely during combat. But because leg techniques are not easy to control, the potential for injuring the partner is there because of the power of the legs. Thus one has to be extra careful when training Wing Chun kicking.

In the beginning of Chow Sifu's teaching career, he was hesitant to include leg technique within the training of sticking hands. It was later through Grandmaster Yip's encouragement that assured Chow Sifu of the value of leg techniques in practical usage. The assurance from Grandmaster Yip ensured that this special aspect of Wing Chun is preserved within Chow Sifu's lineage.

Chapter 6
Conclusion

6.1 Way of the Willow Revisited
In the book we have covered the learning and practice of Wing Chun as taught by Grandmaster Yip Man to Chow Sifu during the middle period of Grandmaster Yip's teaching career.

As explained and illustrated earlier in the book for the Wing Chun practitioner to use Wing Chun without reliance on brute strength he has to be like the willow tree that is able to yield during a powerful storm.

6.2 A conceptual Approach
The Wing Chun approach of Grandmaster Yip Man as taught to Chow Sifu is a very conceptual approach to the question of dealing with conflict in the midst of combat.

By being a very short and condensed system of combat, Grandmaster Yip's Wing Chun system is able to focus strongly on the key points governing the use of the body and effective techniques for implementing martial strategies.

This is because in a real fighting situation factors such as timing, speed, impact, pain, fear etc etc all come into play. An elaborate movements takes more time to complete and every additional second taken also means that the opponent has more time to react.

By keeping it short and simple, the Wing Chun practitioner is able to keep his mind on the objective which is walking out of the situation alive and with minimal injury.

6.3 Limited Approach, Unlimited Application
The limited number of forms when compared to other traditional systems of martial arts does not mean that Wing Chun falls short of or lacks variety in techniques to cope with different forms of attacks.

By understanding the key points of attack and defence the Wing Chun man can effectively use his limited repertoire of techniques to cope with any attacks by changing the height, angle and position of his defending limbs. In this way the Wing Chun practitioner is able to allow his mind and body to freely express the universal truths in combat.

We hope that this book has given the reader an in-depth understanding of the par excellence approach of Grandmaster Yip Man's Wing Chun which Chow Sifu learned it and transmitted to future generations.

Appendix 1
Examples of Applications

Application 1 – Lap Sao-Punch (Photos 1 – 7) :
Tor Bo by rear leg | Shoulder path | Application of Lap Sao-Punch
S : Sifu Donald Mak on the right side
O : Opponent on the left side

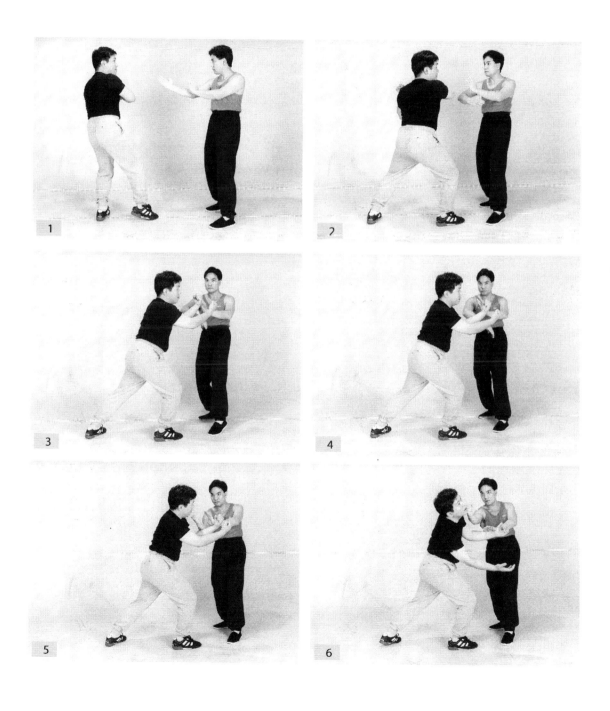

7

1. S and O both at ready position, S Bai-jong, places his right hand in front of his left hand sitting on the Pien Sun Ma

2. O advances and attacks S with a double hanging punches;
S Tor Bo by using the rear leg to shift to his right side in order to move his body from the path of the strong force.

3 – 4. S shifts himself to the left side of O and defends himself by using the low Bong Sao to block O's left punch coupled with the shoulder path alignment

5 – 7. S changes his Wu Sao (left) - low Bong Sao (right) to Lap Sao (left) – Punch (right) on O's head

Application 2 – Pai Jarn (Photos 8 – 13) :
Triangular footwork- Complex pattern and Biu Bo
Shoulder path | Application of Pai Jarn
S : Sifu Donald Mak on the left side
O : Opponent on the right side

8

9

10

11

12

13

8. S and O both at ready position, S Bai-jong with Low Bong-Wu Sao sitting on the Ching Sun Ma

9 – 10. O advances and attacks S with a right tiger claw (Fu-jow). S withdraws his left leg back by Huen Bo and advances with his right leg by Huen Bo-Biu Bo (ie Triangular footwork pattern) in order to move his body from the path of the force to form the shoulder path alignment. At the same time, S turns his right low Bong Sao to right Tan Sao.

11 – 12. S uses the Lap Sao-Pai Jarn on O's rib.

13. It is the view from other side.

Application 3 – Bong Gerk (Photos 14 – 21) :
Triangular footwork | Application of Bong Gerk;
Kau Sao and Low Side Thrust Kick
S : Sifu Donald Mak on the left side
O : Opponent on the right side

14

15

16

17

18

19

20

21

14. S and O both at ready position, S Bai-jong, places his right hand in front of his left hand (Wu Sao) sitting on the Ching Sun Ma. O Bai-jong with a Yuet Ying Sao Gerk (Moon Shadow Hand & Leg)

15 – 17. O advances and attacks S with a right front kick and left round house punch. S withdraws his right leg back and pins his waist to launch a left Bong Gerk to deflect O's right front kick while S's right front hand is in a Chuen Kiu position to guard against O's round house punch.

18. O steps down and continues to attack S with the double punches. S withdraws his left leg back and uses the right Oi Kau Sao to block O's low punch.

19. S turns his waist and lifts his leg. Owing to the advantage of leaning back by putting weight on the rear leg, O's high punch is well guarded by S's left Bai-jong Sao

20 – 21. S thrusts out his right low side kick to stamp at O's left knee

Application 1 – Continuous High Side Thrust Kick and Knee Stamping Kick (Photos 22 – 30) :
Tor Bo by rear leg | Shoulder path | Concurrent Blocking and kicking
Application of High Side Thrust Kick and Knee-Stamping Kick
S : Sifu Donald Mak on the left side
O : Opponent on the right side

28

29

30

22. S and O both at ready position, S Bai-jong, places his left hand in front of his right hand (Wu Sao) sitting on the Ching Sun Ma.

23 – 24. O advances and attacks S with the right curving punch. S Tor Bo by using the rear leg (left) to shift to his left side in order to move his body from the path of the force.

25 – 26. S blocks O's punch with the Kwan Sao and concurrently thrusts out his right High Side Kick to O's rib cage.

27. However, O immediately changes his punch from high line to low line to block S's kick.

28 – 30. S turns his waist and changes his side kick to Knee stamping kick position. Concurrently S changes his Kwan Sao to Bai Jong Sao. S thrusts out his right leg in a slant-straight forward line to stamp at O's right knee.

Application 5 – Man Sao & Dap Sao (Photos 31 – 39):
Tor Bo by rear leg | Triangular Footwork - Basic | Guai Chung (Elbow going back to centerline)
Simultaneous Block & Strike | Application of Man Sao and Dap Sao
S : Sifu Donald Mak on the right side
O : Opponent on the left side

37

38

39

31. S and O both at ready position, S Bai-jong, places his right hand in front of his left hand sitting on the Pien Sun Ma. O Bai-jong with the left Dan Fu Jow Fa (Single Tiger Claw)

32 – 33. O advances with the triangular footwork and uses Man Sao to probe the opponent;

34 – 35. O grabs S's hand and shifts himself to the left side of S and punches on S

37 – 39. S Tor Bo by using his rear leg in order to give himself more room for changing other techniques. At the same time, S turns his elbow (left) back to the centerline (Guai Chung) and changes to Dap Sao to block O's punch and simultaneously punches on O's head.

Application 6 – Fak Sao & Low Gang Sao (Photos 40 – 45) :
Cross leg | Guai Chung (Elbow going back to centerline)
Simultaneous Block & Strike | Application of Fak Sao and Low Gang Sao
S : Sifu Donald Mak on the left side
O : Opponent on the right side

40

41

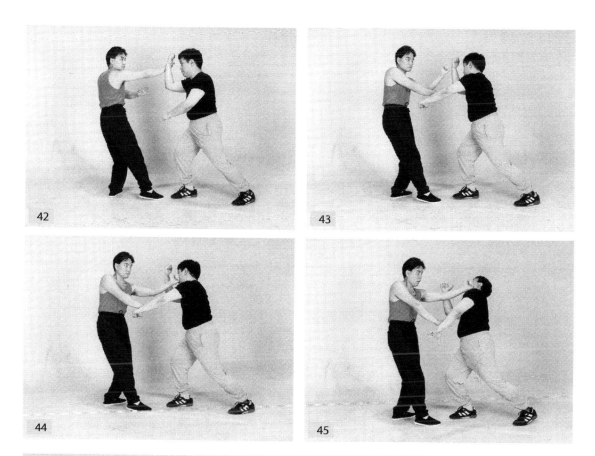

40. S and O both at ready position, S Bai-jong, places his right hand in front of his left hand sitting on the Ching Sun Ma

41. S places his left leg in the cross leg position and advances with the right leg and get ready to attack O with the Fak Sao.

42. O blocks S's Fak Sao and counter strike S by the low line punch; S pins his waist and simultaneously turns his elbow back to the centerline in order to avoid the force from the opponent's blocking.

43. S pins his waist further to have a proper Ching Sun Ma to face the opponent and get himself ready to receive O's counter punch.

44 – 45. S uses the low Gang Sao to block O's counter punch and simultaneously punch back on O's head.

Application 7 – Knee Stamping Kick (Photos 46 – 53) :
Cross leg | Shoulder Path
Application of Gum Sao, Low Gang Sao and Knee-Stamping Kick
S : Sifu Donald Mak on the left side
O : Opponent on the right side

52
53

46. S and O both at ready position, S Bai-jong, places his left hand in front of his right hand (Wu Sao) sitting on the Ching Sun Ma.

47. O advances and attacks S with the right elbow strike. S pins his waist to absorb the incoming force and uses the Gum Sao coupled with the shoulder path alignment to block O's elbow strike.

48. S moves his left leg to the right in the cross leg position. O advances with his rear leg to form the Kei Lun Bo.

49 – 50. O uses the tiger claw to attack S's groin. S blocks O's attack by Low Gang Sao and gets ready for the Knee Stamping Kick.

51 – 53. S thrusts out his right leg in a straight forward line to stamp at O's right knee.

Application 8 – Chuen Kiu-Front Kick (Photos 54 – 60) :
Shoulder path | Tor Bo by front leg
Triangular Footwork – Basic | Concurrent Strike and Kick
Application of Bong Sao and Chuen Kiu-Front Kick
S : Sifu Donald Mak on the right side
O : Opponent on the left side

54
55

56

57

58

59

60

54. S and O both at ready position, S Bai-jong, places his right hand in front of his left hand sitting on the Pien Sun Ma

55. O advances and attacks S with a left hanging punch; S changes his right hand for the right Bong Sao to receive O's attack.

56. S defends himself by using the Bong Sao to block O's left punch coupled with the shoulder path alignment.

57. O continues to attack S with his right Kup Chui; S Tor Bo by using the front leg to shift in front of O.

58 – 60. S raises his left hand from below through the indoor area of O (Chuen Kiu) to block O's Kup Chui, while launching a right front kick at the abdominal area of O.

Application 9 – Gang Sao-Sweep Kick (Photos 61 – 66) :
Cross leg | Shoulder path | Concurrent Strike and Kick | Application of Gang Sao-Sweep Kick
S : Sifu Donald Mak on the left side
O : Opponent on the right side

61. S and O both at ready position, S Bai-jong, places his left hand in front of his right hand (Wu Sao) sitting on the Ching Sun Ma.

62. O advances and attacks S with the left hanging punch.

S moves his left leg to the right in the cross leg position coupled with the shoulder path alignment to get away from O's direct attack.

63 – 65. S raises his right leg to launch a Sweep-kick at O's leg, while S's arms posing as Gang Sao, are striking on O's left arm.

66. It is the view from other side

Application 10 – High Side Thrust Kick (Photos 67 – 72) :
Cross leg | Application of High Side Thrust-Kick
S : Sifu Donald Mak on the right side
O : Opponent on the left side

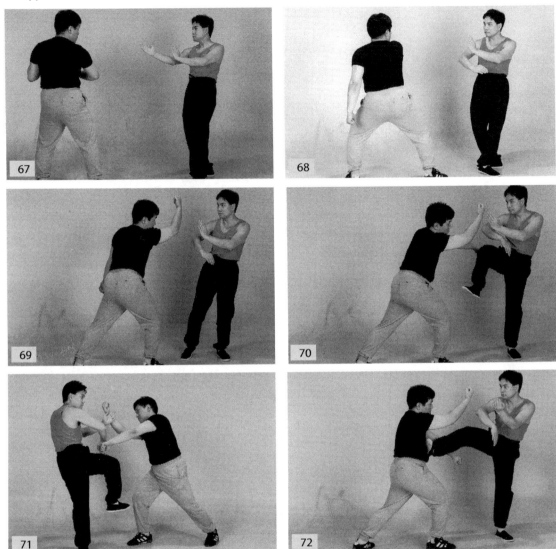

67. S and O both at ready position, S Bai-jong, places his right hand in front of his left hand sitting on the Pien Sun Ma
68. O is ready to launch his right hanging punch and S turns his left foot outward to make the cross leg position.
69. O advances and attacks S with a right hanging punch and left straight punch. S moves his right foot forward getting ready for the side thrust kick.
70 & 71. S raises his right leg while protects himself with the Kwan Sao. No. 71 is the view from other side.
72. S launches a high side Thrust-kick to the rib cage of O, while posing the Kwan Sao position.

Appendix 2
Roots of Wing Chun

1.1 Early Developments

History is a matter of controversy. A complete and comprehensive history is impossible. As such we will limit our introduction to the roots of Wing Chun to only our lineage of the Wing Chun system.

Our late grandmaster Yip Man wrote in "The Origin of Wing Chun" that the art of Wing Chun began with Yim Wing Chun of Guangdong (Canton), China. She had learned the art from Ng Mui, the abbess of the Shaolin Temple in Henan (Honan) who hid in the White Crane Temple in Tai Leung to escape persecution from the Ching government.

Ng Mui taught Yim Wing Chun martial art to enable her to defend herself against a local bully who insisted on having his way with her. Yim Wing Chun defeated the bully after a period of training and went on to marry her true love – Leung Bok Chau.

From Leung Bok Chau, the art now renamed Wing Chun, was passed down to Leung Lan Kwai who taught it to Wong Wah Bo of the Hung Suen travelling opera company. It was during this period that Wong Wah Bo exchanged his knowledge with Leung Yee Tai who had learned the 6 ½ point pole from Abbot Jee Sim.

1.2 Fatshan Leung Jan

Leung Jan was renowned as one of the foremost Wing Chun master in his time. His life and deeds have been immortalized by the author "I-am-Mountain-Man" in the famous historical pulp "Fatshan Jan Sin Sang" (Mr Jan of Fatshan). Leung Jan was said to have taught his son Leung Bik and a few disciples. Leung Jan was said to have taught his disciples to play the pipa before even starting their Wing Chun training to enable them to first loosen their wrists. However it was Chan Wah Shun who was destined to become Leung Jan's most famous pupil.

Leung Jan's Old House at Heshan

1.3 Chan Wah Shun

Among those that Leung Jan taught later in his life was Chan Wah Shun who was nicknamed Wah the Moneychanger. Chan Wah Shun was said to have learned Wing Chun initially by peeping through the fence of Leung Jan's abode when Leung Jan was instructing his students. Later he was accepted by Leung Jan as a

Chan Wah Shun's Tomb at Shunde

student. Chan Wah Shun taught a number of limited disciples including his son Chan Yui Min , Ng Jung So and Yip Man. Yip man was aged 11 at that time. From Yip Man thereon sprang the roots of the Hong Kong Wing Chun system.

1.4 Pivotal Role of Leung Bik

Though it is mentioned that Leung Jan taught Wing Chun to his second son Leung Bik, we know little of Leung Bik. However it has been written that Yip Man learned from Leung Bik after the then young Yip Man lost in a match to the elderly Leung Bik. It is unfortunate that today we cannot trace what has happened to Leung Bik or that he was ever in Hong Kong. This lack of historical record has cast doubt on the story of Yip Man learning from Leung Bik.

Sifu Chow does recall that during his discipleship, Yip Man once mentioned that he had learned from Leung Bik but did not elaborate further. Sifu Chow further recalls that couplets were hung in his kwoon at Lee Tat Street stating his learning from Chan Wah Shun and Leung Bik. He forgot the exact wording of the couplets. Why the figure of Leung Bik is so interesting is that Yip Man attributed the refinement of his advanced skills under the tutelage of Leung Bik.

1.5 Wing Chun in Hong Kong

Different reasons have been forwarded for Yip Man's permanent migration to Hong Kong where from his once exalted position as the son of the wealthy class he descended to be another unknown face among the sea of poverty. Recently another it has been suggested that Yip Man was forced to leave China not because of the coming of the Communist government, but because he killed a person with a kick during a match.

Whatever the reason for leaving his homeland, Yip Man would have been another statistic in the immigration figures except for martial artists such Leung Sheung, Lee Man and Lok Yiu who recognised the skills of Yip Man and asked him to be their teacher at the Association of Restaurant Workers of Hong Kong.

From this small start in 1950, another class was later opened in Stanley Street in 1951. This was the beginning of the spread of the effectiveness of the Wing Chun system as a combat art through challenge matches. During this time students from outside the restaurant trade also joined in. In 1955, Sifu Chow joined the Yip Man's class in Lee Tat Street, Yau Ma Tei.

By 1957 the school had moved to Li Cheng Uk Estate in Kowloon from Yau Ma Tei. Many of the early students had already left Yip Man to open their own school by this time and due to the distance from central Hong Kong, few of the early students came to visit as frequently. The backward living conditions did not help; basic necessities such as water had to be carried from a common tap. Sifu Chow who was working as a bus driver brought in a number of workers from the transport union to join the school. 1961 saw a final move to Castle Peak Road where Yip Man taught until his retirement.

Group Photo of Yip Man after class in Li Cheng Uk Estate in 1957

In 1972 Yip Man passed away from throat cancer and the Wing Chun world lost a living treasure.

Yip Man's Hong Kong Students

1.6 Legacy of Yip Man

Today the seeds that Yip Man sowed once upon a time in Hong Kong has spread far and wide throughout the world. Most of the Wing Chun practitioners worldwide can trace their roots back to Yip Man.

Yip Man's Group photo

1.7 Family Tree

As far as the Chow Tze Chuen lineage is concerned, our wings have not spread as wide as Sifu Chow has kept a pretty low profile throughout his entire teaching career, preferring to concentrate on passing on his knowledge of the Wing Chun system to the next generation until his recent retirement.

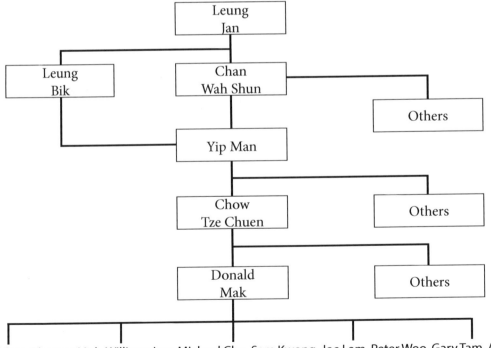

Sarfield Ng, Thomas Mok, Williams Lee, Michael Chu, Sam Kwong, Joe Lam, Peter Woo, Gary Tam, Amos Lau, Jerry Yip, Ida Ip, Andrew Hung, Kam Poon, Lionel Roulier, Adam Gerken, Anatoly Beloshchin, Adrian Tautan, Simone Sebastiani, Robert Kenneryd, Michele Lavino, Mohsen Basou, He Jian Lin, Ruan Guang Ming, Lin Yan Jun, Zeph Wong, Thomas Cheng, Ann Li and others.

Sifu Donald Mak's Hong Kong and Overseas Students

© International Wing Chun Organization Sweden

46799467R00055

Made in the USA
San Bernardino, CA
15 March 2017